HOLY DISRUPTION

A MANIFESTO FOR THE FUTURE OF FAITH COMMUNITIES

AMY BUTLER
DAWN DARWIN WEAKS

FOREWORD BY BRIAN D. MCLAREN

chalice
PRESS

Print: 9780827215184

EPUB: 9780827215191

EPDF: 9780827215207

ChalicePress.com

Praise for *Holy Disruption*

"In this brave, bold book, Amy Butler and Dawn Darwin Weaks challenge the church to step up to its authentic vocation of interrupter of 'business as usual' with both proclamation and enactment of the coming of God's good rule among us. They see such a vocation as an act of hope that summons the church, in its many local settings, away from conventional practices of safety and domestication to exhibit the neighborly love of God in effective, concrete, and public ways. Their appeal is grounded in their clear discernment of the gospel but also in actual practice of discipleship that they identify in many unnoticed venues. *Holy Disruption* has the additional asset of a study guide whereby congregations can reflect on their own faith practices in their own local circumstances. Our thanks to Amy and Dawn for their prophetic perspective!"

■ Walter Brueggemann, theologian and author

"With vulnerability, grace, and courage, Amy Butler and Dawn Darwin Weaks share their journey, experiences, and wisdom in *Holy Disruption*. As many churches face declining membership and challenging decisions—including the possibility of closing—this book offers adaptive strategies to help faith communities reimagine their purpose. By embracing change, churches can become holy disrupters, bringing hope and renewal to a broken world."

■ Grace Ji-Sun Kim, author and theology professor at Earlham School of Religion

"Beyond a collection of truly exhilarating stories, *Holy Disruption* is a workbook for faith communities ready to ask the question, *what's next?* and say to the Spirit, *we are listening*. Butler and Weaks implore followers of Jesus to disrupt our laden notions of institution, ecclesiology, and what it means to serve God and neighbor while offering the Church an imaginative petition: the ground is fertile if we are willing to scatter some seed."

■ Lauren Lisa Ng, Berkeley School of Theology

"Butler and Weaks ask out loud what we are all thinking, 'What does it mean to be the church?' What sets this book apart from others is their answer—Holy Disruptors! Readers will learn the various ways holy disruption is biblical and leads to flourishing. We all need to be disruptors, and this book shows us the way."

- F. Douglas Powe, Jr., President, Phillips Theological Seminary

"It's sometimes said that the church needs to move from creeds to deeds. But Pastors Dawn and Amy are calling us to make those deeds seeds that will spring forth in new life for the church. The creeds tell us that death must come before resurrection. The church must not only confess that faith but profess that hope by creating resurrection models of surprising kinds. 'Imagine,' they say. And then they help us do just that."

- George A. Mason, Senior Pastor Emeritus, Wilshire Baptist Church, Dallas, Texas

Contents

For Rosalie Beck
with deep gratitude for the holy disruption
she gifted both of us and so many others.

For the stunningly brave people
whose stories you are about to read.

And, in memory and honor of our teacher and friend,
Walter Brueggemann, whose theological voice is
woven throughout this text.

Foreword

By Brian McLaren

I suppose on one level, my favorite writers are ones who make me feel good. They massage me with familiar words. They bolster my confirmation bias to protect me from uneasy considerations. They are as comforting as a lullaby and a blanket to a baby … or a cup of hot chocolate to kids fresh from playing in the snow … or an oldie song to a senior citizen. These writers comfort me and make me smile.

But on another level, my favorite writers are the very opposite. Their words nudge me like elbows from the slumber of my previously scheduled complacency. The sharp points of their paragraphs deflate my biases like pins in so many brightly colored balloons. Their chapters are like buckets of ice water dumped on someone who has passed out drunk … or like a "Hey, watch out!" shouted to someone about to step into traffic. They make me wince, but in a good way.

Having awakened me, they point me where I need to go next. In this book, Pastor Amy and Pastor Dawn show both the generosity and kindness of that first kind of favorite writer … and the courage and clarity of the second. Their intended audience is clergy, denominational leaders, and equally, committed lay people … people who care about churches and worship and community and mission and the like. Their task is not to barrage you with bad news. They assume you know that already, even if you act as if you're in denial. They understand something about you. You have a reason for pretending that you don't know the bad news about the great spiritual disruption that is here or coming soon in nearly all of our churches. Your reason? You don't know what to do about the great disruption. So you don't think about it or talk about it.

What you need, your authors realize, is permission to imagine … to imagine both new wine and new wineskins … to imagine new expressions of faith, community, and mission … to imagine God doing a new thing. That's why your kind and candid authors take you on literary site visits in these pages, to meet real people in real places who are exploring what to do next, preparing for life after this great spiritual disruption that is shaking our ecclesial institutions. The places you will go are amazing. The people you will meet are even more amazing. And the creative work they are doing ... more amazing still.

So Pastors Amy and Dawn don't offer you comfortable denial in this book: how could they, when the word *disruption* is in the title? Nor do they offer you the false hope of quick fixes that won't work. Nor do they offer you despair or nostalgia or distraction or someone to blame. Instead, they offer you imagination, along with a dare ... a dare to believe that this great spiritual disruption unfolding around us could lead to a great spiritual re-imagination ... and in so doing, make the disruption truly holy.

On a very personal level, I'm so glad that Pastor Amy and Pastor Dawn have written this book. I was a pastor for twenty-four years, and after that, I wrote books and traveled the world trying to help pastors face the disruption wisely and in time. But in the last few years, I've come to the conclusion that too few of our leaders and institutions have been ready, willing, or able to do what needed to be done in time. If there ever was a chance to turn the downward trajectory of the church in the West in general and the U.S. in particular, I think the window of opportunity has passed.

Renewal is less and less of an option when most of our congregations are either a) going over a demographic cliff, with average ages passing sixty, seventy, and eighty ... or b) selling out to right-wing and reactionary political movements ... or c) both. This realization has created a problem for me. Most clergy and lay leaders didn't read my books or invite me to speak to tell them about disruption and resurrection. They wanted me to be one of those comfortable writers who sang to them with lullabies of reassurance ... to tell them that renewal was possible, that it could be painless, and that it could happen fast, before they spent their savings or buried their last members.

I did my best to give them hope, but I couldn't lie. No, I had to tell them: renewal wouldn't be painless; it would be almost as painful as dying, maybe more! No, renewal wouldn't happen quickly; it would take more time than they had, so they had to plant trees that would bear fruit for their children and grandchildren, but not them. No, change wouldn't be easy: it would require rethinking everything, from theology to polity to liturgy to community to mission.

Pastors Dawn and Amy have started where I left off: reminding us that there is something even more powerful than renewal, namely, resurrection. They tell the truth: resurrection doesn't happen without death first, and death doesn't happen without dying first, and dying is not easy. In other words, yes, there is life and hope after this great spiritual disruption. But no, there are no shortcuts. Yes, faith communities have a future, but no, it is not the future most of them imagine, namely, a return to the 1950s or 1980s or 2000s or whatever.

I remember speaking in a Lutheran church one weekend, and the pastor came up to me afterwards and said good-naturedly, "McLaren, you are a nice guy but you are so naive."

"I am sure you're right about the naive part," I said, laughing. "But I guess I am too naive to know where I am being naive. Help me." "You think we in the institutional church are interested in transformation. But no, here's what we're interested in: preservation. We just want to preserve what we've got until we die. We in the institutional church will spend the rest of our lives micro-managing our own decline."

Remembering his words—honest, even if painful—makes me wish I had a copy of this book to give him. I could have said, "Ah, but even so, our churches could be like mature trees. They could start producing seeds that the wind will carry far and wide. They could start investing their energy and assets in the new wine and new wineskins of tomorrow, even as the church of yesterday declines. Here's a book that could help you imagine what that could look like."

So that's the book you're holding. Remember: it's not trying to give you "the answer." It's trying to do something much more important. It's trying to seed your imagination.

Who knows where that could lead? ❖

Walk around feeling like a leaf.
Know you could tumble any second.
Then decide what to do with your time.
—Naomi Shihab Nye[1]

[1] Naomi Shihab Nye, "The Art of Disappearing," in *Words Under the Words: Selected Poems* (Portland, Oregon: Far Corner Books, 1995).

CHAPTER 1

No Shortcuts

Humility is a virtue. Unfortunately, gaining it often involves the experience of being humbled. Organized religion is experiencing a long-anticipated comeuppance in the United States. Religious institutions as they have been for about eighty years are becoming shadows of their former selves.[1] Large buildings that used to house bustling crowds are now mausoleums; vibrant youth groups are increasingly rare; and task forces on what to do next are becoming plentiful. The mantra of "try harder, work more, and keep going" has limped away, defeated by questions that are no longer tamed by any answers we know.

Just twenty years ago, 46 percent of Americans attended religious services weekly. Now, 30 percent do.[2] Currently in the United States, churches that close each year outnumber new church starts by 50 percent.[3] At least 4,500 churches are closing here annually.[4] How humbling. How painful. We wish that we didn't have to see this discouraging decay before new life breaks forth. It's just plain human

[1] Jeffrey M. Jones, "Church Membership Falls Below Majority First Time," Gallup, March 29, 2021, https://news.gallup.com/poll/341963/church-membership-falls-below-majority-first-time.aspx.

[2] Jeffrey M. Jones, "Church Attendance Has Declined in Most U.S. Religious Groups," Gallup, March 25, 2024, https://news.gallup.com/poll/642548/church-attendance-declined-religious-groups.aspx.

[3] David Roach, "100,000 Reuses for the Church to Find," *Christianity Today*, September 25, 2023, https://www.christianitytoday.com/2023/09/church-buildings-size-sale-development-multiuse-empty/.

[4] "Study: More Churches Closing Than Opening," *Religion News Service*, March 26, 2021, https://religionnews.com/2021/05/26/study-more-churches-closing-than-opening/.

to wonder: Why can't we go from glory to glory, like the apostle Paul promised?[5] We feel a little like our friend who lamented the death of a loved one. She cried out, "I know one day I will have some peace again, but can't anyone tell me a shortcut to getting there?"

We're in uncharted territory. We know so little these days about what faith communities are becoming. What we do know is what faith communities are *not* anymore. We know that what we've considered success in past iterations no longer meets that description. Large sanctuaries with crowds of people listening to grand organs, boisterous volunteer choirs, and heady, manuscript preachers are now dwindling. The privileged influence of being "the place to be" at 10:50 on Sunday mornings with plentiful volunteers to fold the bulletins and make the coffee … it's all going, going, gone, and it has been for some time.

And as our institutions wane, we can't help but secretly wonder if that fading mirrors our faith, making the grief we're navigating extraordinarily heavy and nearly paralyzing. We wonder: *What about the vows I made at the altar when I got married? All my children were raised running through these buildings! This is the place that helped me navigate some of the deepest grief and pain of my life. Who am I—who are we—if the institutions we so closely associated with God do not exist anymore?* This disruption of church as we know it can make everything feel shaky and uncertain.

It's not that we intentionally would choose devotion to a familiar institution over faithful change that creates hope. It's just that what we have known as faith community for so many generations has been a source of comfort and belonging our whole lives long. But times have changed, and the way we create, tend, and live in faith community has changed radically, too. The season for wistfully hoping for a return to what was is over.

We think it's time to name our insistence on church and institution as we know it as sin. Idolatry, even. Now is the moment to speak the truth about where we are so that we may begin to imagine a fresh path that will take us where we may have never dreamed.

[5] See 2 Corinthians 3:8.

As people of faith, we have a story of good news about the new life that is possible after death. Once upon a time, God became a human being named Jesus who taught us that a seed that falls to the ground and dies will bear much fruit.[6] Then he showed us that truth in his life, teachings, death, and resurrection.

A seed that falls to the ground and dies? Perhaps in the heyday of our institutions, we weren't paying enough attention to these parts of the biblical witness. A story about falling to the ground and dying, after all, doesn't sound so appealing. But what if our inability or unwillingness to embrace this truth alongside the bustling activity of the church nursery caused us to miss a very critical part of the teachings of Jesus?

Ignoring the necessary death that precedes resurrection has been a sin of the modern church. Somebody needs to help us embrace this moment of comeuppance, empty pews, and emergency task forces as opportunity instead of only grief, as a holy disruption instead of just harrowing dying. So as closure comes to our old way of churching, we, Pastor Amy and Pastor Dawn, die-hard clergywomen, are looking in unlikely places for the beginnings of new life that Jesus taught us always comes after the dying.

When we saw each other last year at a clergy women's gathering in a coffee shop, we started talking about what our unrelenting prayers were for this moment in the Church. We shared stories of courageous, out-of-the box ideas being implemented by imaginative and brave leaders. Out of lament and longing, we began dreaming of cowriting a book to tell some of these stories to crack open more possibilities for what is next for the future of faith communities.

We're both in our third decade of pastoral ministry, the persistent daughters of the Church who were told to bide our time and put in sweat equity until, one day, the Church would be ready for women like us to lead. Now that we can lead in some roles, the task of religious institutional leadership is far more complicated and far less esteemed than it was for the men who came before us. But we have

[6] See John 12:24.

determined not to give in to sell a prosperity gospel or a religion of cultural acquiescence just to fill the seats again; that was not what Jesus, nor the congregations that formed us, taught.

We are still here in the faith communities that shaped us, eagerly searching out what comes next. Since you're reading this book, maybe you are, too.

In our grief and utter stubbornness (faithfulness?), we refuse to believe the emptying of pews and the shuttering of sanctuary doors is all there is left for American faith communities. Instead, we believe, as Jesus taught us, that these moments of despair are seeds that, even after death, can spring up with the hope of new life.

So we are taking courage to search for what comes next. We've got our eyes trained on signs of life emerging in unlikely places, perhaps even in the very places where death was the only thing we could see. We're preaching, pastoring, and praying for a resurrection-level imagination, both for ourselves and for the people who make up our faith communities. And in this book, we're asking:

- What's next after this disruption?
- What might a community shaped by the gospel—a faith community—look like next?
- What does it take to share genuine faith and compassion with our neighbors in this moment in the history of Christianity?
- Where and how do we find the courage to look for what we believe to be true: life springing forth out of death?

In this book, we are asking our readers to meet the challenge of American religious institutional decline with a courageous and faithful imagination. We invite you to prayerfully envision what the blessing of new life might be on the other side of death.

We're pleading with you to join us. Use your imagination. Open your mind and your heart to possibilities you may not even have considered before—to holy disruption.

***

Often, when Jesus wanted to help us develop our spiritual vision so we could see how his presence among us would take shape, he told stories. Stories engage our minds in new ways and prod our exploration of courage and faith. When he wanted to explain something, for example, Jesus would say, "The reign of God or the kingdom of heaven is like ..." and then the story he told would catch us by surprise. He would depict systems and traditions we've become far too familiar with, turned on their heads. He would disrupt our old ways with his new ones, rooted in ancient truths. What he preached required courage—looking outside the easy, expected answers and opening our eyes and our hearts to welcome something different.

According to Jesus, a vibrant, world-shifting Kingdom of God is perhaps not what we thought it would be or maybe even what we wished for—an empire swooping in to vanquish evil and give us power, ease, and wealth. If we listen carefully to Jesus, we'll begin to realize that the coming world he described is like wheat and weeds that grow in the same field and are left alone until all can be sorted out at harvest time.[7]

The reign of heaven is like a tiny mustard seed, barely visible until it grows to a big enough plant for birds to find their homes in it.[8]

God's dream for the world is like a reckless farmer who throws seed everywhere and is delighted with their unlikely return, aware that his work is only to throw the seed and the end result belongs to God.[9]

Jesus showed us that stories take us beyond where we have gone before and lead us very often to the most unexpected places. So, to help spark your own faithful imagination, we too will tell stories—stories of holy disruptors doing the work of creating life where it seemed death was the inevitable end. We'll tell stories of people challenging what we thought church had to be and stretching our understanding of what faith community can be now.

---

[7] See Matthew 13:24–43.

[8] See Mark 4:30–32.

[9] See Mark 4:1–20

Here you'll read stories of people on intrepid expeditions to live into questions about what's next for the future of faith communities—stories of people who left what the institution *normally* looked like to see what it *could* look like, with or without permission to do so, and stories of people willing to risk everything to do exactly what faith calls us to do: love and care for our neighbors. These innovative, holy disruptors are social entrepreneurs,[10] doing exactly what Jesus both did and taught. They are planting seeds in places traditional institutions have overlooked or cast aside, or simply no longer have the capacity to consider serving. The people you'll meet here might not call themselves particularly gifted, but many of them are. What they share is the tremendous grit it takes to turn grief over institutional decline and death into an opportunity to look ahead toward even the smallest and most unexpected signs of life … in the most unlikely places.

Their stories begin in England and take us to LA's Skid Row, to Maui, to St. Louis, to a bee sanctuary, to a dialysis lab, and to an abandoned strip mall. These stories will shine a light on tiny sprouts of life, emerging unexpectedly, throughout the most intractable institutional structures. You'll meet people living out their faith in unorthodox yet unmistakably holy ways, people opening grocery stores in systems of food apartheid[11] and creating faith community on theater stages. We'll even share a bit of our own stories of experiences of holy disruption as we begin.

You'll get to know congregations who boldly connect their resources with their religion and their buildings with their beliefs. You'll meet people of faith who are witnessing God's spirit turn what some might call wildly, even irresponsibly, flung seeds into job training centers and restaurants for those in need. You'll remember what Jesus kept trying to teach us: *of course* the presence of God lives and thrives

---

[10] Social entrepreneurship addresses community problems through ethical business models, giving faith communities opportunities to expand their outreach and income streams in nontraditional ways, as well as to foster an economically healthy and generally thriving community. In short, social entrepreneurs work to do good and to do well at the same time.

[11] "Food apartheid" is a term used by hunger-relief activists to depict intentional, systemic inequalities of access to fresh, nutritious food that especially impact non-White communities.

beyond traditional institutions. You'll remember and celebrate that, truly, where there is good, there is God.

These 21st-century faith stories help us believe what we should have known all along. Death really is the gateway to new beginnings, the gospel is still wildly effective when set free to do its work, and God isn't anywhere near done with us yet. A small group guide at the end of the book will help you connect insights from these stories to your own unique story, as well as ask you to pray some terrifyingly hopeful, courage-filled prayers. Maybe you and your faith community already are or will become holy disruptors, too.

If you read this book looking for a step-by-step guide for how to pass over the hard lament of dying to move back into an easy, familiar, traditionally comfortable existence again, it's likely you'll be woefully disappointed. But if you read this book open to honing an unfurling, sanctified imagination based on evidence that Jesus is still rolling back stones and calling for the dead to rise, we're hoping you'll be radically inspired. We want you to read this book and finish it eager to see more, to be more, and to create more.

We must not be afraid to say that the Church as we have known it is undergoing a shift that likely will result in a new way of living out our faith—a way we may not even be able to imagine. We cannot yet see a full picture of what is coming next. But we do know that the work of God, always creating healing and wholeness in the world, does not stop when our institutions flag.

In these moments of uncertainty, we're suggesting that the holy disruption now underway, demonstrated by the innovators you'll meet here, is a place where new life is emerging. This is joyful confirmation that God isn't finished with us yet. Faith is not waning. Faith is alive and thriving—its roots growing deeper and wider, extending far beyond the walls of the church and planting itself in every corner of our communities. And while what the future of the church will look like is not yet clear, perhaps our most faithful response in this moment of uncertainty is to step into unknown territory with courage and to become holy disruptors ourselves.

Disruptors, rebels, or maybe even prophets—the voices you'll hear are voices up ahead inviting us to follow, to move all of us toward change and wholeness and God's promise for a better world. As you read the stories of these leaders, keep in mind the definition of a prophet Walter Brueggemann offers: "Prophets are called by God to have an impact on persons, to impinge upon perception and awareness, to intrude upon public policy, and to evoke faithful and transformed behavior."[12] Their voices are among a whole chorus calling us to look up from our grief and fear to catch a glimpse of some new possibility we never thought of before.

As you read, you'll notice that we defiantly refuse to equate closing institutions with the absence of God's healing work in the world. We invite you to join us in that refusal. Perhaps together we will become a group of holy disruptors who move with courage into the call of this moment. Maybe we will bid goodbye to what has been so that what we were always meant to be can unfurl: agents of new life for ourselves, for our neighbors, and for our world, to the glory of God.

There is no shortcut to glory in this strange institutional moment of grief-filled goodbyes and tenuous hope of new life. But hear the good news: there is much holy adventure, experimentation, and innovation stirring among faithful people who know that life does, in fact, come after death.

You're invited here to an expansive theological vision of what church is becoming next. In the chapters that follow, we'll first briefly share some of our own death-to-life stories before we introduce you to some amazing people who are radically repurposing resources, blessing their neighbors, creating communities, and changing unjust structures. As we read and imagine together, perhaps we can become the kind of holy disruptors Jesus liked to tell stories about, people unafraid to live into the story that undergirds all we say we believe: that abundant, world-changing life always, always comes … after death.

---

[12] Walter Brueggemann, "The Book of Jeremiah: Portrait of the Prophet," in *Interpreting the Prophets*, eds. J.L. Mays and P.J. Achtemeier (Minneapolis: Fortress Press, 1987) 117–18.

Those who believe in God can never in a way be sure of him again. Once they have seen him in a stable, they can never be sure where he will appear or to what lengths he will go or to what ludicrous depths of self-humiliation he will descend in his wild pursuit of [us]. If holiness and the awful power and majesty of God were present in the least auspicious of all events, this birth of a peasant's child, then there is no place or time so lowly and earthbound but that holiness can't be present there, too. And this means that we are never safe, that there is no place where we can hide from God, no place where we are safe from his power to break into and recreate the human heart because it is just where he seems most helpless that he is most strong, and just where we least expect him that he comes most fully.

— Frederick Buechner[1]

[1] Frederick Buechner, "Frederick Buechner: A Face in the Sky, Christmas Day," day1.org, December 24, 2019, https://day1.org/articles/5dff79606615fbce3a000021/frederick-buechner-a-face-in-the-sky-christmas-day

CHAPTER 2

Diving into Disruption

The first time I saw the buildings, I knew. To me, Pastor Dawn, our old church buildings were a beloved mess. The boiler didn't work; there was no elevator to the second floor; the halls were too narrow; there was no main, accessible front door for guests to find; the parking was grossly inadequate—I could go on. When my husband and I came to interview to be co-pastors for First Christian Church (Disciples of Christ) in Odessa, Texas, we were simultaneously wooed by the congregational leaders' chutzpah and discouraged by the church's location and physical plant. "We will be your co-pastors," we told them, "but you don't need us to pastor this small group. You can take care of each other if it is just going to be the forty-five or so of you."

"But," we told them, "we will come be your pastors if you are willing to boldly move into a relocation and a new start to your ministry to reach your community again." In essence, we said, "We are not called to be your caretakers. But we *are* called to be your disruptors." Much to our surprise, the congregation said yes and let's go! Then we had to make good on our promise to meet their courage with our own.

We moved our family across the country and entered a challenging, three-year, intentional decision-making process with the church. It was not easy to think about stepping away from the stained glass and the organ and into the great unknown. Harder still was to ask the Holy Spirit if our unique mission of bringing the inclusive gospel of Jesus Christ to an area where hardly any churches were doing that was even worth the risk. But soon the vast majority of the congregation agreed: the future was calling us. It was time to let those buildings go and make a new beginning in ministry. Thank the Maker the congregation had the spiritual maturity to release what had once served them and their neighborhood but no longer did.

A few folks thought we were reckless to sell our traditional space and give something new a try. Shortly after the "for sale" sign went up, I received a phone call from a disgruntled granddaughter of a deceased patriarch of the church. She no longer attended our church nor gave any money herself, of course, but she complained: "My grandfather gave a lot of money for that church to stay right where it is!"

Think about that statement for a moment.

I knew old churches could transform and thrive because I'd seen it before in my ministry. This is my third century-plus-years-old congregation to pastor. The first also relocated; the second nested a new church within its campus; and the third is the relocated, renamed, repurposed, revived congregation I serve right now. Congregations can be resilient and be born again and again. Or, of course, they can stagnate and stay stuck.

If your goal is to keep a church "right where it is" for as long as possible, you may have forgotten that we serve a risen Christ who would not stay put in a sealed tomb. He is risen and on the loose in our world! Remember when Jesus showed up after his resurrection and appeared to the disciples, even though they had locked the doors?[1] If our faith communities are anything like Jesus, we will be on the move as well, showing up in unexpected ways and places.

Thankfully, the life-giving Spirit of God took our congregation out of our buildings and into a new adventure of following Jesus. Imagine: On the second Sunday of Eastertide in 2017, we voted to sell the beloved old buildings and purchase a medical office building and dialysis center. Talk about putting our trust in resurrection to the test. The disruption was palpable, painful, and thrilling, all at once.

We stayed in the old buildings another six months getting ready to stuff a century of ministry into a moving van. Our last day to worship in that sanctuary was the Sunday after Christmas. The music was still

---

[1] See John 20:26.

all carols like "Away in a Manger," "Joy to the World," and such. I thought the service was going well enough and even had some joy in it. I admired how these folks were being so brave as we jumped into the unknown together. This was almost fun!

Then the offering came. Our pianist played "Go Tell It on the Mountain," and we started passing around the old brass offering plates we kept out of the moving boxes for just this occasion. I was singing along to the carol—"Down in a lowly manger, the humble Christ was born … "—but I was interrupted by a strange sound. Clink, clunk. Clunk, clink. It was not the normal sound of change hitting the metal plate; it had a heavier timbre than that.

It continued intermittently until a deacon brought the plates to the front. It was then I saw what had created the noise: it was keys! Keys in the offering plate! Our faithful church leaders were releasing their keys to the building where they had served Christ for so many years. They were doing this one last, hard thing. They were truly letting go.

Now their hands were empty and ready to embrace whatever God had for us next. Unbidden tears came as I fished my own keys out of my purse and added them to the offering of our bittersweet release.

Disruption is hard, but it can be extraordinarily holy.

For over a year, our faith community met for worship in an elementary school cafetorium while we renovated our new-to-us building. Soon we had repurposed, relocated, and relaunched a vibrant ministry growing from the well-established roots of our congregation.

We are now a 119-year-old church with a new name—Connection Christian Church—a new location, and a renewed purpose and reputation in our community. Within our current building is the "Connection Center," where we host five local nonprofit organizations in office spaces and shared community rooms in a special synergy of resources. All week long, we are a hub of ministry, from receiving clients in a community counseling center, to hosting trainings for Big Brothers Big Sisters mentors, to being the designated community disaster relief shelter in partnership with our local American Red

Cross. With God's help, we have positioned ourselves to be uniquely inclusive and unabashedly oriented toward serving our community, embodying that in our physical building. Because of that, we are the first call for everyone from the fire chief to the food bank when our neighbors need help.

It was a risk to throw all of those seeds out, let them land, and see what happened. But this is the needed risk for many, if not most, of American congregations at this moment. As described more fully in my previous book, *Breakthrough*,[2] Connection Christian Church (Disciples of Christ) is now a thriving faith community of three hundred people and growing as we constantly care for our neighbors and innovatively use the resources we have. What a gift that our congregation didn't just stay put.

***

Taking steps toward a fresh expression of faith is always sure to disrupt institutions and systems we were taught were our holy responsibility to save. Over and over, we have experienced firsthand the pain of disrupting tradition; as women in a field traditionally dominated by men, much of our professional experience of representing and implementing change has been filled with powerful pushback.

To be fair, by our very existence working in a system built to undergird the leadership of men and the traditional structures of American society, we have been pushing back at foundations that seemed totally inviolable or systems that seemed to be fine just the way they were, thank you very much. After all, institutions are called "institutions" for a reason. To call something an institution is to set it firmly in an intractable, cemented foundation. We do this, in part, to prevent (or at least to mitigate) substantial change that might result in uncertainty.

To object to institutional shift is a very human and reasonable response to change: "I like how things are. I do not want to learn a

[2] A full version of this story can be found in: Dawn Darwin Weaks, *Breakthrough: Trusting God for Big Change in Your Church* (St. Louis: Chalice Press, 2002).

new way. I do not want to be uncomfortable. I will therefore build a scaffolding that will prop up the reality in which I feel the most at ease. I will create an institution." We do this with religions, of course, but we also do it in government and even in our own personal lives ("the institution of marriage," for example). And institutions serve us well … until the world around us shifts, and the institution we'd come to depend on doesn't fit the reality we're living so well anymore.

I, Pastor Amy, will never forget my first few months as a newly minted senior pastor at Calvary Baptist Church in Washington, D.C. The lore and legacy that floated in the air at Calvary was almost tangible. Presidents and Supreme Court justices had been members, and prominent D.C. movers and shakers still held sway, even in their eighties and nineties. In this beautiful place, "institution" was inviolable, and even the suggestion of substantive change was threatening—disruptive. I realized this a few weeks in during a meeting of the Board of Deacons. The board was responsible for worship, the weekly anchor of the church's life. And to invite the community to worship, the deacons did as they had done for many decades: they printed an ad in the Saturday edition of *The Washington Post*.

It made sense. Many of those who served on the deacon board recalled their own experience of moving to Washington, D.C., as young professionals decades before. They'd been taught by dutiful parents that one of the first priorities of moving to a new city was opening the newspaper on Saturday, finding the religion page and the ad for the closest worshiping community of their denomination, and showing up for worship the very next day. This was, to most on the board, an essential part of institutional expression.

Even in 2003, I found this practice antiquated at best, and when I discovered that the church was paying $900 a year for two lines a week in an obscure corner of *The Washington Post*'s religion page, I suggested that we cancel the ad and direct that money instead to creating a welcoming website that displayed all the information for worship on Sundays.

The deacon board was, to put it mildly, aghast. How would new people in town know where to go to church if there was no ad in the Saturday edition of *The Washington Post*?

I was a young leader who did not appreciate the extent to which my suggestion upset the longtime leaders of the congregation. But by the same token, I knew that the younger visitors the congregation sought would not be checking the newspaper for worship times, so I pushed (too ardently, a more seasoned pastor might have advised) toward the change. One of the deacons resigned on the spot. But we ended up getting a newly designed website.

This instance was a memorable moment of personal shift from a church leader as institutional caretaker to a leader who felt a deep calling to be a disruptor of institutions. Caretaker, I think, is a softer path than disruptor because the experience that must happen when it's time for institutions to shift, for what seems inviolable to be challenged, for something to end so something new can be born, is upending and threatening, and it hurts.

Humans generally don't like disruptors because disruption challenges institutions and requires us to move from what feels safe and familiar to something different. And while institutions can and do serve us, what we propose here is that *the way of Jesus is a way of holy disruption, of looking beyond what does not serve our mission effectively anymore and focusing instead on something strangely unexpected.*

That deacons' meeting led me to gain a nickname in the congregation: the deacon chair Howard dubbed me "The New Orleans Flash," as I'd come to the church from New Orleans. There's not a doubt in my mind that the pace of disruption I introduced at Calvary made many people uncomfortable; I often had an end goal in mind and moved forward at a pace that did not fully appreciate the delicate balance between tradition, comfort, familiarity, and the necessary disruption God's Spirit brings whenever She does Her work.

Eventually (and often painfully) I learned a little more about why the rhythms of church life felt so sacred and untouchable to some while others had a higher tolerance for change. And I eventually became convinced that the only way any group of people emerges on the other side of necessary disruption is through building trust and sharing a common goal.

As our community moved toward this new way of being the church together, we endured some difficult church business meetings, the kind of meetings that everyone leaves shaking their heads and saying, "I can't believe people at church act that way." It wasn't easy in the least, but little by little we got there. Every Sunday we'd begin worship by reciting our mission statement: "We are an ecumenical, multiracial, multi-ethnic, Christian body that reaches out to the world with the good news of Jesus Christ. To that end we strive to be welcoming, responsive, trusting, and prayerful in everything we do."

It felt some Sundays like an unnecessary and repetitive exercise, but I knew it was making an impression when those terrible business meetings began to ease, when trust took root and began to grow in the space between tradition and innovation, and when we experienced the truth that disruption isn't only loss. We were discovering that change can be like an adventure, like setting out on a journey toward something new with some of the people you love the most.

While I'm sure my appetite for change still made Howard and others startle from time to time, together we found a pace that suited our community. We'd try something new and trust each other in the trying, we'd forgive each other when we made mistakes, and we'd shake our heads in celebratory disbelief when God showed up in the middle of everything.

And that's what I eventually began to believe a community of faith should always be: a place where we have to practice actually having the faith it takes to live into the ever changing, always creating work of God in the world. Somehow at Calvary we'd managed to build together a community where most everybody was okay with a little discomfort from time to time, and in which we'd choose again and again to trust each other and most of all to trust God's beautiful, disruptive choreography.

The delicate dance soon became second nature. I couldn't imagine my life without a community of faith with which to face the changes always just around the corner, without people I loved and who loved me to walk through it all together. Disruption without a community magnifies the fear of change.

Despite that conviction and the experience I lived at Calvary, six years later I found myself alone—without community—in the middle of a seismic shift in my life that I never saw coming. Call it naivete or the arrogance of certainty or some combination of both, but my vocational path disrupted the comfort and beauty of the community at Calvary when I was called as the pastor of another church. This new job catapulted me into a bewildering and very public role as pastor of the Riverside Church in the New York City. It was a disruption of the highest order, but I knew a shift in community could happen—I'd seen it and lived it.

To be fair, five years of leadership at the tallest church in America did engender significant change in that congregation—a disruption to their image of what a leader looked like, for a start. I was the first woman in that role, and perhaps more disruptive, I desperately wanted to offer to this new congregation the possibility I'd seen take root at Calvary. Over and over I preached what I knew was possible and oh-so-beautiful, sounding a newly rigorous call to become a community that saw disruption as possibility and differing opinions as a holy challenge to learn to work together, with each other and with God.

And while we know that disruption and dis-ease are not why people generally come to church, welcoming the possibility change brings is integral to following the wind of God's Spirit. I could see it happening, and if we could ride the waves of change, I felt sure we could build beloved community at Riverside, too.

And yet, despite the tremendous change for the good, the new faces filling once stagnant pews every week and possibility around every corner, fear won the battle as it so often does. Perhaps there wasn't enough trust between us to navigate the disruption; maybe the pace I set was too rigorous. Even now, years beyond the painful ending of our relationship as pastor and congregation, I still wonder how it was that we couldn't seem to embrace together the beautiful disruption to which God was calling us.

This ending meant, of course, the beginning of something altogether new. And so it was that I found myself, for the first time in my entire life, without a community of faith to walk with me into an unknown future. It was a disruption of the highest order, and it felt many days like I had barely enough light to see my next step and sometimes not even enough courage to get out of bed in the morning.

It was during this period of unrest and disruption in my own life and journey that I unexpectedly found myself accepting the invitation of a friend to get away, far away, to go to England to rest and recover. I needed to try to have the courage it would take to pick myself up, dust myself off, and begin again to put my hand to the work of holy disruption. London welcomed me with the gift of anonymity and a blustery, gray November that matched my sadness but wouldn't let me stay mired in my despair.

There was, after all, still a world desperately in need of healing, and somewhere underneath all the evidence to the contrary, I knew there had to be others who had lived the truth I knew: that holy disruption is often the way by which God invites us into new life.

For nothing is fixed, forever, forever, forever, it is not fixed; the earth is always shifting, the light is always changing, the sea does not cease to grind down rock. Generations do not cease to be born, and we are responsible to them because we are the only witnesses they have.

—James Baldwin[1]

[1] James Baldwin, "For Nothing is Fixed," in *Nothing Personal* (Boston: Beacon Press, 2021).

CHAPTER 3

Planting the Seed

Opening the door and walking into the streets of London in October felt like the whole world was inviting me, Pastor Amy, to embrace change. Colorful leaves tenaciously clinging to tree branches in neighborhood parks finally gave in to the tug of the breeze and floated to the sidewalks, painting trails of beauty.

Some days the sun would sparkle off the Thames almost mischievously; most days were damp and gray—reminders of the winter ahead and invitations to slip into the pub on the corner and find myself wrapped in the warmth of neighbors gathered.

London became my greenhouse for starting over after having been dismissed and discredited by an institution I had poured every part of myself into righting. Despite the pain and disruption in my life and the lives of such a beautiful congregation, I still had so much to learn about how *holy* disruption—the upending of what felt comfortable and steady—could spur us on to a deeper and more impactful expression of our faith. In between the grief, I undertook the process of exploring where communities of faith might thrive in the middle of change; I'd become curious about how social enterprise—businesses built to do well and do good at the same time—was bolstering these communities, specifically in Great Britain.

Institutional religious organizations in London (congregations that served their communities with social and spiritual support programs) were on a journey of rediscovery ahead of their counterparts in the United States. For several decades already, the realities of empty churches and dwindling congregations had challenged people of faith in Great Britain to imagine new ways of being the "Church." They had already become adept at living the mandate to love God and love neighbor when changes in their institutions required them to think outside the box.

I wanted to wander through these creative projects: cafes and cleaning companies, coffee shops and fine dining restaurants, community gardens, and commercial kitchens. I wanted to see and experience these expressions of faith community. I wanted to find answers to some questions that had been on my mind for well over a decade.

When religious institutions that define our lives undergo such profound change, the impact of that change always takes us by surprise. Experiences we understand to be infallible seem suddenly to shape-shift, and along with institutional change, our hearts become uncertain, too. We begin to wonder about questions we wouldn't or couldn't ask aloud: *If the church changes, does what I know to be true about God change, too? Everything around me is changing radically; why can't the institution that represents my faith stay the same?*

I've always engaged my faith community the same way: 11 o'clock Sunday morning, fifth pew on the left, right next to the stained-glass window installed in memory of my grandmother.

What does my faith mean? Who is God? How do I live my faith in the world if the way I always did it just doesn't exist in the same way anymore?

For three months in London, I walked into change every day. I met pastors running bakeries, coworking spaces, and culinary training programs. I saw communities gather in pew-less sanctuaries to share a meal with neighbors on Friday nights. I met people running thriving businesses while paying workers a living wage.

And every time I walked into one of these spaces, I was welcomed into conversation or introduced to an idea I'd never thought of before. I was challenged to wonder if the idea of "church" I'd been trained to build and lead was less of a responsibility to tend the holy grail and more a stranglehold that would not allow me to feel the cool breeze of change. It felt like many other moments of profound shift in my life: an invitation to look in unlikely places for courage to embrace something new.

One afternoon in a pub in London, I sat at the bar with a man I would meet that day and never again, at least not yet. I was there to hear the story of something he'd called "seedbed." Seedbed was not an organization or a nonprofit; it wasn't an institution or even a legal entity. It was a significant gift of money entrusted to him by a wealthy friend who had invited him, more than two decades before, to "find something wonderful" to do with it.

A person of deep faith and a leader in the world of social enterprise, this man built a small network of trusted friends all over Great Britain and assigned them a task: look around at your community, find the businesses that are having social impact and solving social problems, and go to coffee with their leaders. Hear their stories, find out what motivates them, listen to what they need, and help give money away.

This loosely connected effort began and continued for twenty-three years. Upon hearing the stories of these business owners, my new friend gave small grants, enough for a commercial oven, funds to secure a storefront, or payment to buy a sign for the front of the business. They were little grants, given with no strings attached, to affirm and support the work of social entrepreneurs making the communities of Great Britain places where loving your neighbor was lived out every day.

As our time together was wrapping up, this man looked at me and said something that would change my life: "It's been twenty-three years, and we just gave away the final disbursement of that fund. Looking back over these years, I can tell you this: almost every single social enterprise that is now thriving in Great Britain can trace something back … to seedbed."

The reaction I felt to his words in that moment was physical; it was less like the sparkling Thames River inviting me to come see and more like a gusty London wind pulling me toward something that would change my life. All of the wondering about church and faith and changing the world focused immediately on what I'd studied in seminary and preached for so many years: the seed parables of Jesus.

Jesus told story after story about seeds—about how tiny seeds become huge trees, about the profound faith it takes to believe a seed in the darkness of the dirt could amount to anything, or about how opening our fists to toss seeds of goodness into the world is fundamental to being a person of faith. In this moment, I suddenly saw all of Jesus' seed stories as fundamental to being the "Church."

What a gift our robust religious institutions of the twentieth century have given us: the foundation of considerable assets by which we can seed the world with goodness. Assets that include tradition, history, stories of our faith, buildings, and so many gifts we can share with the world, if only we can begin to move beyond our fear.

My friend got up to leave our meeting that day, and I left to walk a few blocks in London, back to where I was staying. When I returned home, I couldn't shake the image of a seedbed, particularly the utterly disruptive idea of finding people trying out interesting ways of healing the world and giving them resources and support to keep trying. I already knew from personal experience that living life as a disruptor demands a high price. It's hard to sell a new idea, and when that idea pushes back at convention, those leading the innovation are often collateral damage when institutions resist the work of innovators. Still, what if we created an effort, like a seedbed, to support the work of innovators addressing the decline of religious institutions in the United States?

Invested Faith[1] was born out of this experience. Invested Faith is a fund established to receive the assets of institutions nearing completion—the end of their institutional lives—and to redirect those assets toward the work of faith-rooted social entrepreneurs building businesses that are challenging unjust systems.

In other words, faith communities that reach their completion can send a powerful message through collaboration with Invested Faith.

[1] An appendix with more detailed information about Invested Faith is included at the end of this book.

Resources gathered and tended over many decades of life together remain, even if neighborhoods change or congregations decline. And that means completed communities of faith can still have powerful impact in their local communities as well as communities across the country. Invested Faith exists to remind people that God's work in the world never ends and that embracing the change we face can be a powerful act of witness.

It was Jesus himself who taught us this, if you think about it. There isn't an overabundance of passages in the gospels describing Jesus' membership on a committee or attendance at temple business meetings. The stories we read are, instead, stories of a lover of people who didn't seem bothered by bucking convention and trying something new. We most often find Jesus out on the hillsides or on the deck of a boat or sharing a meal with shady characters at the home of someone with a bad reputation.

It's not that Jesus didn't lament the challenges in the organized religion of his time; I think he would understand the sadness and fear of change in American faith communities. In Luke 13:34, as he was entering Jerusalem and facing increasing danger, Jesus said of the city almost wistfully, "Jerusalem, Jerusalem, the city that kills the prophets and stones those who were sent to you! How often I have wanted to gather your people just as a hen gathers her chicks under her wings. But you didn't want that."

But you'll notice if you read Luke 13 that Jesus' wistful longing for tradition cannot pull his eyes away from the reason he was there in the first place: to teach people how to love God and love their neighbors in ways that change the world. With currently over seventy Invested Faith Fellows we've found on the "hillsides and boat decks and dinner tables" of our country, a powerful network of those who believe and act boldly with the conviction that God is still vibrantly at work has emerged and continues to grow.

Where we are does not look like where we have been. But God is here, perpetually beckoning us to step outside our easy assumptions and courageously show up in unlikely places to offer the resources we have to meet the needs all around us—to love God and love our neighbors, in other words. The courage and action of congregations and faith communities at their completion are critical to continue identifying, resourcing, and connecting Invested Faith Fellows as the network grows larger and stronger. Completion—death, some call it—is never the end. Perhaps, in fact, it is only the very beginning.

This is the central story of our faith.

***

Now it's your turn. We invite you to imagine what holy disruption might look like for you in your life, in your community, in the world. In order to awaken that imagination, here we introduce you to some very bold changemakers. Let their stories stir your heart to courageously open to the possibility of holy disruption that is an invitation to newness and possibility.

The people you're about to meet are Invested Faith Fellows[2]—let's call them holy disruptors. They are radically repurposing church buildings and resources available to them; blessing their neighbors with empowering initiatives; creating new communities of support and growth; and, in short, disrupting systems of dehumanization and changing the world. Imagine from their stories what might be possible from your own story, starting with how people of faith might open wide our hands to release traditional church assets and allow new life to begin again.

The stories you will read here are stories of only a few of the many brave changemakers we've encountered, people making use of social innovation to live out our shared mandate of healing the world. There are simply too many stories to tell them all, but they represent an entire movement. Our aim in telling them is to ignite a spark in your heart and your community, a spark that grows into yet another story we could have told in this book or perhaps might be told in another.

---

[2] You've read the basic idea behind Invested Faith, and we've included an appendix at the end of this book with more details.

You'll notice as you read that we've organized these narratives around four themes: (1) radicalizing our resources, (2) blessing our neighbors, (3) growing our communities, and (4) disrupting unjust systems. In truth, each of these stories has elements of all these themes. Each project we recount is a response to the brokenness of the world; each uses creative methods and pushes boundaries to try something new. And each in its own way mirrors the rabbi who walked the hills of Galilee turning a picnic lunch into a community meal and a terrified and ashamed tax collector into a proud dinner host.[3] As you read, watch for new life springing up in unexpected places and see if you can see that seed growing amidst your neighborhood, your faith community, and your call to heal the world.

---

[3] See Matthew 14:13-21; Luke 19:1-10.

We have to be braver than we think we can be, because God is constantly calling us to be more than we are.

—Madeline L'Engle[1]

[1] Madeleine L'Engle, *Walking on Water: Reflections on Faith and Art* (New York: Convergent Books, 2016), 58.

CHAPTER 4

Radicalizing Our Resources

You may notice that, sprinkled throughout this book, including in the title, we've chosen to use words meant to jar, maybe even startle a bit. Disruption, manifesto, and now radicalizing ... you may be asking, why the need for such provocative language? There's a method to our madness, as the stories you'll read in this chapter and the chapters ahead should challenge the ways you've been thinking about faith, community, and even your own resources and how you use them. In this chapter you'll meet some holy disruptors who took a look around at what they had and began to think outside the box about what to do with it.

Humans love routine and institution; we generally resist change. In the case of institutional resources we've experienced one way our whole lives, we may not ever have considered that the way we've always used buildings and endowments and parking lots might need to shift. Institutional change is some of the hardest to make and to live through. Shifting the use of institutional assets intended for use in one way to be used in another way altogether can be very uncomfortable. But maybe take a deep breath before you dismiss what seems like a radically alternate way of thinking about our resources. Dare to open your heart to consider the stories of these leaders who saw possibility in congregational resources when others could only see decline.

Imagine: Rev. Katie Kenyon was out mowing her lawn one day. Trying to get the yard work done in between raising her two young children, fulfilling her role as full-time associate pastor, navigating her divorce, and caring for a foster child was a tall enough order. She managed to keep juggling all the balls without dropping one most of the time. But that day the lawn mower choked and ground to a halt. It was broken. And something inside Katie broke, too. She was somehow, somewhat managing until that moment. Katie realized she didn't have anyone nearby to ask for help. She didn't know her neighbors, and her extended family lived far away. She didn't know where to take the mower to get it fixed or how she would pay for it. She walked inside the house and tried to make the shift to start preparing dinner. But she couldn't do it. She remembers wondering, *Is this how it all ends?*

She began to be curious and ask herself: if she felt this isolated as a minister at a church, someone who "should" have a community of people she could call upon, how many other people were feeling alone and defeated by life's daily challenges? For Katie, that moment was the seed that changed everything. The uncut grass in her front yard somehow planted something in her heart—an urgent need to find a way to create community for and with others.

It wasn't long after Katie's lawn mower died that somehow, miraculously, a way to tend that seed in her heart showed up on her doorstep. A church in her town of Richmond, Virginia, was seeking a better use for their building. Like so many religious edifices, the facility was going unused other than on Sunday mornings. The once large, now small congregation was rattling around in the building wondering the same thing Katie had asked after her lawn mower broke: *Is this how it all ends?* They wanted to make a bigger difference in their community and didn't know how. All they knew was that they had this big building to offer to assuage the gaping needs in their community.

The church reached out to Pastor Katie for help, and she agreed to consult with them using her expertise in social work and ministry. She thought she might help them get started with a meaningful outreach plan in a few coaching sessions. But before long, Katie knew this was the response to the calling she'd received that despair-filled afternoon in her front yard. Soon, Village Green RVA was born to disrupt neighbors' isolation with a caring community.

Village Green leases space for one dollar a year from the church, which allows them to offer offices to organizations serving the community, coordinating with more than sixty community nonprofit organizations, churches, and government agencies. Together they provide wrap-around care to anyone in need and offer daily volunteer opportunities filled by neighbors who want to support each other. The "village green" once had been a place where neighbors came together to be connected. Village Green RVA is making that a thing again.

Not your typical charity that gives a handout and sends you on your way, Village Green's goal is to connect you into a community. If what you need is help with your lawn mower, or a referral for a mental health need, or simply a listening ear, that's what they do. Just show up, and someone is there for you. Daily meals are prepared by a chef to be ready to eat on the run. Weekly meals are offered there in the facility, served up family-style for anyone in need. You can even swing by on your way home from work to pick up dinner for your family and, when you do, give a donation to provide dinner that night for a family who might be hungry.

Now that once quiet church building bustles all day every day of the week, and the people of the original congregation are there, giving of their time and talents to create community for their neighbors. And not just them, but legions of volunteers from throughout the city of Richmond. It is an authentic community bringing together people across economic and ethnic divides. It is church every day of the week. Reverend Katie gives the help she once needed to others with a whole lot of partners alongside her. Katie says people come to Village Green to be seen. How is your congregation at seeing people and networking to meet their needs?

***

Imagine: The wall of the church parlor where Rev. Chelsea Spyres works boasts historic, black-and-white photos of the church's previous, somber-looking male pastors. But now for Pastor Chelsea and the four churches[1] that make up the Wilmington Kitchen Collective (WKC) in Delaware, it's a full-color future ahead. They have figured

---

[1] The four Wilmington, Delaware, churches include Grace Church, First and Central Presbyterian Church, Aldersgate United Methodist Church, and Westminster Presbyterian Church.

out how to gather people in the community to experience the love of God in nontraditional ways. Chelsea's dream and calling have always been about gathering diverse people around welcoming tables in the name of Jesus.

She was once a case manager for folks experiencing homelessness. She yearned to connect more of her faith and her faith community into her work. Now she partners with churches who are yearning to connect more of their faith with their community. These days, her congregation is made up of the people she pastors at Riverfront Ministries and the food truck entrepreneurs coming in and out of WKC's kitchens in four churches.

The Wilmington Kitchen Collective is all about disrupting the quietness of many church buildings during the week to create a place of belonging for the community in church kitchens. As you probably know, church kitchens are often large and even commercial-grade, and to say most are underused is an understatement. But not these church kitchens. They are being used to build a community of food truck entrepreneurs. Many of the hustling, hardworking business people who run food trucks work on weekends when churches normally meet, so the Kitchen Collective brings church to them. WKC staff serve as chaplains to the food truck chefs and their assistants, checking in on them in person when they are cooking and via text at least monthly. Community that draws us together is powerful in its own right; those of us who invest our lives in faith communities experientially know that. And building a business alone can be isolating and fear-filled. As food truck operators use kitchens and interact with clergy and other leaders of WTC, slowly, slowly the loneliness wanes.

Chelsea says that often they were just looking for a kitchen and didn't fully realize they also got a faith community when they signed on. But as relationships formed, they started to feel like family. The established congregation members have become customers, and bridges are being built between diverse folks that would have never been built otherwise.

WTC offers business development classes, networking, and advertising support to the entrepreneurs. Best of all are the quarterly potlucks that vendors and congregation members hold. The food is to die for, and the connections made across the tables are the stuff of heaven. Rev. Chelsea couldn't have guessed that this is how gathering people around the Lord's table would look, and when she sees it now, it is better than she could have imagined. There are forty food truck operators on WTC's waiting list. Expansion and growing ministry impact is unlimited. How often is your church's kitchen used? What would it look like if the reign of God sent a shoot up out of the unlikely ground there?

***

Imagine: What's happening in your sanctuary when it's not Sunday morning? How about theater rehearsal? Jon Adam Ross earned his acting degree from New York University's Tisch School for the Arts. An accomplished actor, he is also a deeply committed community leader and arts advocate. Jon Adam's passion is poured into the Inheritance Theater Project. ITP is a powerfully effective interfaith, national nonprofit arts organization that produces original theater cocreated and performed by neighbors who may have been in conflict with one another.

When community leaders invite ITP to their neighborhood, the organization teams with local artists to tackle perplexing issues, from local disputes to national problems, with inclusive and justice-centered community building. Every show has a sacred text as its foundation. Cast and crew wrestle with the text and its meaning in conversation with folks living in the community. They engage in a participatory playmaking process, writing the play as they navigate a divisive civic issue together. Creating and presenting a theatrical production turns into an opportunity for bridge-building.

ITP often uses sanctuaries and houses of worship for this work. These sacred spaces are fitting vessels for art that provides connection for people across divides. There, together in a house of worship, the community addresses root problems like racism, corruption, and distrust, and neighbors are invited to participate in the artistic process while addressing real-life, time-sensitive, civic challenges. Each ITP residency lasts between nine and twelve months. During that time leaders cultivate relationships and hold open rehearsals that invite feedback so that the show that is eventually presented to the community is accurate and authentically connected to the people it represents. The performances are pay-what-you-can, with all proceeds going to local organizations to continue the bridge-building work.

One community in Nebraska invited ITP to help them make sense of community tensions around the influx of refugees to their neighborhoods. Nebraska has one of the highest per capita populations of resettled refugees in the nation due to demand for labor from the meatpacking industry. Omaha area faith communities St. Augustine of Canterbury Church in Elkhorn, Nebraska, Hanscom Park Methodist Church, Trinity Episcopal Church, and Beth El Synagogue hosted the project in hopes they could find a creative outlet for misunderstandings in the community. The resulting original play, called *Exodus: Resettlement*, explored themes of the biblical Exodus narrative integrated with local exodus stories both recent (newly American refugees from Sudan) and historical (the Omaha tribe that was forcibly expelled from what is now the City of Omaha).

Though the curtain has fallen on the show itself, the more than twenty-five local community organizations that came together in those months in 2019 continue to foster a growing relationship with each other as they work together to serve their community. The performances raised funds that went to Lutheran Family Services Office of Refugee Resettlement to help provide grants to artists who are new Americans recently resettled. And it all started with letting a theater company move into the church sanctuary. Jon Adam says that a nation divided is looking for tools that build bridges. How might your sanctuary be one?

***

Imagine: Drew Nagy read *The Human Phenomenon* by Jesuit priest Pierre Teilhard de Chardin while he was in seminary, and it changed his life. He always felt drawn to nature, and as a Christian, he knew that God had created the earth and tasked people to care for it and all its inhabitants. But through de Chardin's work, Drew felt the calling to ecojustice, integrating ecology with spirituality and activism. He never imagined himself as a traditional pastor, and now his path was clearer to him. Drew took a job as a part-time youth minister at Westover Baptist Church in Richmond, Virginia, and began teaching math at a private school as well. Somehow in his spare time working two jobs, he became a beekeeper and planted a community garden. He imagined starting an urban monastic community where people were invited to live in harmony with the land, keep a daily spiritual rhythm, and enjoy hospitable space for contemplative practices.

A Baptist monk? Drew knows it sounds a little strange. But the concept of people living at the church in communities is as old as the Nicene Creed.

As the congregation at Westover Baptist Church declined and experienced other changes, Drew became the congregation's lead pastor. He and the congregation entered a conversation about how to be better stewards of their increasingly unused forty thousand-square-foot building and three acres of land. As the church's need for room for themselves diminished, the possibilities for all their space could become for their neighbors lit a fire in the congregation's imagination.

Today, Westover hosts Living Water Community Center, which includes a bee sanctuary, a monastery with full-time residents and many guests who stay for various lengths of time, a community garden, a coworking space, and wellness programs including yoga and martial arts.

The church transformed the upstairs wing of the educational building into residential space and decided three acres of grass to mow was not the most creative use of the land God had entrusted to them. They are now expanding their housing by remodeling their building to host even more people for long- or short-term stays. Some of their new neighbors have been previously homeless, others are retired and longed to live in community, and some intentionally chose to be shaped spiritually by monastic living.

All of the residents have the opportunity to work in the garden, around the church, or with the bees, defraying the labor costs of the congregation. They also participate in the rhythm of daily prayers, and some join the congregation for worship and Bible study on Sunday mornings. The congregation's small circle has been disrupted by their bountiful hospitality and willingness to be home for strangers who become friends. Together, Westover and Living Water Community Church are living the ancient concept of an abbey . . . in a Baptist church.

***

Imagine: A coffee roasting company producing delicious coffee while paying a living wage to people having difficulty finding decent employment because of the time they spent in jail. Meet Rev. Dustin Mailman, founder of Deep Time Coffee. Dustin didn't grow up in church. In fact, he was suspicious of Christians, as many are. Dustin grew up aware of how churches can judge and hurt people, something his mother, who gave birth to him at age sixteen, had experienced firsthand.

But then Dustin was invited to attend Camp Tekoa, a United Methodist camp in North Carolina. There he experienced Christ through mentors who introduced him to ministry that included the poor and outcast. When Dustin went to college at Appalachian State University, he became involved in church for the first time. What he found at King Street Church was a congregation intentionally including people of diverse economic circumstances. There, he and other church members met every weekday in a coffee shop with impoverished neighbors they had invited, sharing life for an hour, drinking good coffee, and reading the Psalms.

Dustin remembers how remarkably good the coffee was and how his neighbors who had never had anything but instant coffee responded to the pungent taste. Dustin thought his neighbors seemed to experience a momentary change in self-esteem when they had access to really good coffee. It planted a seed in him as he wondered about the church's role in offering access to good things for disenfranchised people.

After seminary and serving as a chaplain to people experiencing homelessness and mental illness, Dustin was called to be the associate minister at Trinity United Methodist Church in Asheville, North Carolina. The church averaged eight worshippers at the time and hoped Dustin would jumpstart a children's and youth ministry. Dustin set about getting to know the neighborhood by chatting with people in the houses around the church, the people experiencing homelessness on the streets nearby, and those at the dollar store across the street from the church. What he discovered was that this neighborhood was being devastated by the effects of incarceration on employment. Many returning citizens didn't have jobs because of their criminal records, which resulted in downward spirals of drug use and homelessness.

When Phoenix, a woman Dustin had befriended who lived on the streets near the church, died of a drug overdose, he knew. Phoenix was a gifted woman, but as a felon, she didn't get a second chance at being gainfully employed and rebuilding her life. Dustin knew the time had come to start a business that employed returning citizens to give them a second chance at access to a good life. He asked Trinity's leadership to give him one of the empty Sunday school rooms in their gigantic three-story empty building, and he started roasting coffee.

Deep Time was born. Its soft start was in July 2023, and as of January 2025 they were doing five hundred thousand dollars in business annually. Volunteers are plentiful. They lead financial coaching, conflict resolution workshops, Bible studies, and other aspects of the ministry. All of the employees are returning citizens, rebuilding their lives. The church's return on their Sunday school room is a 600 percent increase in worship attendance and the nearly magical appearance of families with children whose parents are drawn to the work of God in Deep Time.

***

All of these stories are stories of disruptors, of people who had the courage to look around at the gift of institutional resources and say, "Maybe we could use these in ways we've never considered before!" And sometimes maybe we can let go of what we've worked so hard to maintain and instead use the assets we've inherited to pivot with the wind of God's Spirit.

Praise the Lord for the imagination and courage to plant seeds and watch to see if they grow! Hallelujah for the Holy Spirit's help to sprout in concrete and break through! Maybe it's repurposing an old building. Maybe it's releasing it to use the assets to fund an innovative ministry elsewhere. Maybe it's something else entirely. Imagine what would happen if you put the seed of your church building and other assets into the fiercely hopeful hands of the Holy Spirit and see what She does with it. Imagine ... how you might open wide your hands to release old church buildings for new life to burst forth from them?

The question which has to be put to every local congregation is this: whether it is a credible sign of God's reign in justice and mercy over the whole of life, whether it is an open fellowship whose concerns are as wide as the concerns of humanity, whether it cares for its neighbors in a way which reflects and springs out of God's care for them, whether its common life is recognizable as a foretaste of the blessing which God intends for the whole human family.

—Lesslie Newbigin[1]

[1] Newbigin, Lesslie. *Sign of the Kingdom* (Grand Rapids: Eerdmans, 1981).

CHAPTER 5

Blessing Our Neighbors

Holy disruptors do what it takes to be an abundant blessing to their neighbors. From impulsively buying a used school bus on Facebook Marketplace to bringing the community together to play dodgeball, some of the most creative, faith-rooted changemakers take their cues from Jesus, who often set tradition aside if it did not serve the needs of his neighbors.

The gospel accounts of Matthew, Mark, and Luke all tell some version of a story of Jesus encountering a man with a withered hand and healing him in the synagogue on the sabbath.[1] His action in that story gained him harsh criticism from representatives of the institution to which he belonged. Even though more healing had entered the world, not everybody celebrated it. This is nothing new to us. Within the very structures that call us to care about our neighbors, we often encounter constraints that discourage—openly or subtly—the introduction of innovation, the going outside the walls of these institutions we've built and tended, in order to more effectively meet the needs of our communities.

And yet we love to tell the stories of a radical rabbi who, after spending a day teaching on the hillside of Galilee, noticed that the people around him were hungry. With the found resources of five small loaves of bread and two fish, Jesus and his disciples fed the whole crowd, with food left over.[2] Exactly how they made that happen is perhaps not the point of this story. Instead, what if the story is meant to challenge you and me to think outside the ordinary and look for God to show up in the most unexpected ways?

---

[1] See Matthew 12:9–13, Mark 3:1–6, and Luke 6:6–11.

[2] See Matthew 14:13–21.

Imagine how people of faith could deeply listen to the needs of our neighbors so we could bless them, discovering seeds for the fruit of new purpose.

***

Imagine: Tiffany Terrell was working in the banking industry after the financial crisis of 2008 hit. While her bank took the government's bailout, she wondered where the bailout was for poor Americans. In 2020 she left banking to serve those in need with her husband, a probation officer. Together they opened an after-school childcare program in an underserved area, implementing his dream of supporting families transitioning out of the criminal justice system.

In the course of their work, they immediately began to observe the lack of access to fresh food for these children; the health impacts they noticed over and over were alarming. Tiffany soon learned just how segregated food is in the United States. She realized that one side of their town has Publix, a high-end grocery store with produce from all over the world, and the other side of town has Dollar General, a convenience store with only canned food and no fresh fruits and vegetables. Out of her concern for the families in her care on the Dollar General side of town, Tiffany went to a conference about food access in the United States. While she was there, she saw a retrofitted van that just happened to be in the area. The van was serving as a grocery store on wheels.

What if we had a bus for these families that would drive fresh produce into their neighborhoods? she thought. So she searched the internet and bought a used school bus on Facebook Marketplace. And Better Way Grocers sprouted up.

More than a mobile grocery store that brings fresh food into areas not served by the systems of food apartheid in Albany, Georgia, A Better Way is nutrition education on wheels. They offer classes to neighbors on how to season food in healthier ways, using onions and peppers instead of butter and salt. Everything in the store is labeled with how it can help your body. For example, cucumbers boast a sign that says "helps regulate blood pressure." Now A Better Way hosts classes for cooking and exercise out of their new brick-and-mortar headquarters. Because of its success, the business has been able to connect with a local unemployment agency to hire an intergenerational workforce whose participants they are mentoring. A Better Way Grocers keeps training and coaching its teams to understand that there is enough and more than enough goodness to go around. Its customers and staff have become like family, looking out for each other and growing healthier together. Together, every day they are feeding the five thousand and disrupting a food system that used to actively harm their neighbors by providing an abundant garden of goodness in its place.

***

Imagine: Jen Owens and her husband served as missionaries to Russia for five years. When they returned to St. Louis, Missouri, they looked for and found a church that emphasized caring for the poor and immigrants, not just occasionally but as a regular part of a Christian life. So when their church asked for volunteers to host a refugee family for a Thanksgiving dinner, the Owens family was glad to do it. Two families who had fled from their home country of Bhutan and lived in refugee camps in Nepal for fifteen years came to eat at the Owens home. The seeds planted from that table years ago were life-changing.

As Jen got to know her new neighbors, she became aware of the challenges they were facing, unlike any in her own life of relative privilege. She wondered what chance they had for a good life in the United States, considering their limited education and English proficiency. She listened for what would be helpful and began offering the women opportunities to craft together and sell their products. Soon Forai (Friends of Refugees and Immigrants) was born.

At first, Jen orchestrated pop-up stores in friends' homes to sell the women's crafts to give them some extra income. Now, some fifteen years later, the jewelry and sewing company she started, Forai, mentors eight to twelve women each year as artisans and administrators working at a living wage. They also take an additional twenty to thirty women under their wing in community sewing classes.

For many new arrivals to our country, the hope they feel at first gives way to disappointment as they encounter hurdle after hurdle for work, health care, transportation, and more. But Forai disrupts that hopelessness by giving women the support they need to begin making a lasting home for their families and themselves. Forai holds offices out of St. John the Baptist Catholic Church, alongside several other organizations working together to serve immigrant and refugee populations. If women think they would find it helpful, they are connected with a mentor who helps them navigate their new life in the United States. Also, Jen and her volunteers invite the artisans to come thirty minutes early, if they would like, before their biweekly educational classes begin. During that time, they share prayer and teach a Bible story in the women's native language and in English. This time of faith development is not required in any way but gives the women an opportunity to understand why Forai exists and to be a part of faith community if they want. Forai is a friend in the name of Christ helping them make connections that feel a little more like home.

***

Imagine: Emanuel "Boo" Milton was a popular radio disc jockey living in his hometown of Baton Rouge, Louisiana. He enjoyed the rapport he had built with the community but knew there was more. He began to feel a deeper pull to be a good steward of the following he had gained in his young life. As he grew in his relationship with God, he realized that God gave him the gift of connection with people. His first effort to turn his local celebrity status into good for the community came with a "Give Back Weekend," in which he invited his neighbors to volunteer locally with various organizations. The response was so positive that Boo started an organization called Cure with Love.

Before long, Cure with Love created several other projects to bless its neighbors, including Spark Box, a social-emotional development kit available to families during the pandemic; Brighter Futures, a community-wide clinic made available to all local children who needed vision care; and the CHILL program, a conflict resolution workshop for youth. The organization continues to spin off projects. For example,

Cure with Love designed and led an initiative that enabled local parks across the city to have Wi-Fi so children had the access they needed for schoolwork during the pandemic. Much of this work is funded by an annual dodgeball tournament, of all things.

Each project of Cure with Love starts with noticing a need in the community. Then Boo and his team make key connections between those who have a need and the people who are already leaders in neighborhood systems. Their goal is ultimately to connect everyday people with resources to help them thrive. It is as if the Baton Rouge area is truly a parish and Cure with Love leaders are its ministers.

***

Imagine: Jessica David was working for a community foundation, putting her master's of business administration to use in fundraising and grant-making. Though she enjoyed her work there for over a decade, a nagging question was plaguing her. She wondered what impact the investments were making when the vast majority of the funds were not staying local but instead being invested in companies on Wall Street. It seemed to her that the problems they were trying to alleviate in making grants in the community were not being solved. Instead, they were being perpetuated by the way the foundation's investments were being made. Seeing this trend, Jessica and five colleagues started Local Return.

The goal of Local Return is to raise money to create investments in Rhode Island so that local businesses, entrepreneurs, and neighborhoods can thrive. Profits are then reinvested in the same community that generated them in the first place. Now, Local Return has created the Rhode Island Investment Cooperative to house the nation's very first "diversified community investment fund" (or DCIF). A diversified community investment fund invests primarily in real estate but also invests in local businesses and can do so with investment capital raised publicly from within the fund's own community, including non-accredited investors. A DCIF distributes profits to community investors, creating a wealth-building opportunity for everyone, while contributing to a growing local economy.

Local Return can provide capital to local entrepreneurs, like a woman who grew up translating for her mother and now runs her own language translation business and a man who runs a company picking up food waste from restaurants to dispose of in ecologically conserving ways. Local Return is disrupting the way wealth is made in our country by investing in people who make a tangible difference in their communities. And they are inspiring communities of faith to ask: How are *our* church's funds invested? Are our investments hurting or helping our neighbors?

Most of all, Jessica and her team are tackling the income inequality that grips our nation and in the neighborhoods where they live around Providence, Rhode Island. They are starting conversations with neighbors, faith communities, and business owners about their values and the impact they want to make with their assets of real estate, stocks, and everyday financial choices. By offering workshops and consultations, they are building capacity in communities for financial knowledge, discernment, and confidence to plan for intentional, positive impacts locally that make building wealth accessible to all.

***

Imagine: Cynthia Daniels was raised in a conservative church that taught her that being an LGBTQ+ person was an abomination to God. But after her teen daughter wrote Cynthia and her husband a letter letting them know she was transgender, Cynthia did her own study and prayer work to discover not just what she was taught but what she truly believes. The Daniels then walked their daughter through her transition at the GENECIS Center at Children's Medical Hospital in Dallas. Their goal was to do everything in their power to show their daughter that they love her and that she was made by God to be who she is. "Everything" included looking for and finding a church that expressed the love of God for them.

In 2023, when Texas' state legislature passed SB14 to end gender-affirming medical care for minors in the state, the Daniels family was watching. Their faith community, Galileo Church, geared up to stand with families who were having their health care stripped away from them. They began with ten thousand dollars in seed money to support families who needed to travel to maintain their child's health care. Soon, the congregation's pastor called Cynthia to lead the North Texas Transportation Network (NTTN). NTTN makes travel funds available to its neighbors in the nineteen counties that make up the North Texas area who have children undergoing medical care for gender affirmation.

When potential grant recipients learn that a church started this ministry, they are often shocked and sometimes suspicious. NTTN disrupts their concept of who Christians are. Recipients wonder why this church is helping them when their experience of so many churches is to be judged and rejected. NTTN is helping to heal families who have been broken by a world that has discarded them, some who have even been investigated by the state for child abuse simply for seeking medical care for their transgender children. NTTN has already helped more than sixty families with grants of two thousand dollars a year while offering them connections with LGBTQ+ support resources in their community, including Galileo Church. NTTN is now beginning moving grants of three thousand dollars to support families who feel it is necessary to move to another state for their children's care and safety. Donations come from around the country for this ministry.

Cynthia says that sometimes keeping the faith is hard, but the "mama bear" instinct is strong. And remembering that God is not a gendered being in the sky but the multifaceted Love who creates, loves, and walks alongside every transgender person makes the fight worth it.

Hallelujah for the Holy Spirit's help to truly hear the cries of our neighbors and for communities that take heart to respond! Thanks be to God for holy disruptors who somehow find the courage to step outside expected norms and traditional institutions to help us see God in the most unusual places. Imagine how you could deeply listen to the needs of your neighbors and invest in their flourishing. Pray to find the courage to set out in a new way, with your community of faith as a seedbed for discovering the wild and unexpected work of God.

They Didn't Know How Hungry They Were

until their neighbors
were handed the fish
and soft round loaves

lips flecked white
with tender flesh
teeth tearing bread

and his followers
burdened by baskets
heavy with freshness

spilling bounty
on the ground

nearly trampled underfoot
the truth

there'd always
be enough

—Michael Lyle[1]

[1] Michael Lyle, "They Didn't Know How Hungry They Were," *Heart of Flesh Literary Journal*, no. 11 (May 2024), https://heartoffleshlit.com/issue-11/michael-lyle/. Reprinted with permission from Michael Lyle.

CHAPTER 6

Growing Communities

What we've learned from these holy disruptors is that it's a mistake, if not a blatant sin, to limit our definitions of faith community to familiar buildings with stained-glass windows and pews, to traditional structures of leadership, or even to rituals that comfort and define our communities. We'd be wise to remember that Jesus spent very little time in institutional committee meetings, necessary as they sometimes are. He didn't even mention writing bylaws to start a new religion. Faith community happened around him, seemingly organically, in all kinds of places; and it always involved relationships, care for neighbors, and a challenge to move toward justice, more easily taken on together.

With what kind of expansive imagination would we live out our faith if we were able to recognize and nurture growing faith communities in places *beyond* traditional church buildings and at times other than 11 o'clock on Sunday mornings?

Imagine: The small church that Beverly Jenkins and her husband, Ken, planted twenty years ago in Missouri has never had a building of its own. They moved from one temporary location to another temporary location as the congregation changed over the years. It was never their goal to own a building, as they preferred the flexibility of moving as their church outgrew space. While they were co-pastoring, they were also running the nonprofit they'd named Refuge and Restoration, a transitional home that helped men previously incarcerated or unhoused, walking alongside these men as they settled into homes and new, healthy lives. All the while, the Jenkins' community of faith remained nomadic until a dream, and a permanent building, became their focus and vision.

An abandoned shopping mall in Dellwood, Missouri, adjacent to Ferguson, sat empty for twenty years. The massive, continuously empty buildings served as proof that few were looking to invest there, especially after the killing of Michael Brown drew attention to the problems and pain of that community and surrounding neighborhoods. The neighborhood around it was exhausted from disinvestment but hopeful for someone to see the area's potential again. A woman who lived behind that mall began praying when the mall closed—a full two decades before the Jenkins showed up. She even drew up a little picture of what she imagined that transformation could look like: a daycare, maybe a workforce training center, perhaps even a church could meet there. Others in her neighborhood also began praying with similar hopes for the abandoned plaza.

Meanwhile, Beverly and Ken regularly drove by the abandoned mall on the way to visit Ken's family. It seemed a shame for the mall to be going to waste like that. Beverly and Ken began to pray together about it, too. Beverly even sketched out some ideas of how the space might be used. The vision was for the buildings to have five pillars represented: early childhood education, workforce development, small business and entrepreneurship incubation, banking and access to capital, and community resources needed by the underserved neighborhood around it.

As Beverly and Ken prayed and wistfully wondered every time they drove past the development, the pull of the possibility practically demanded they begin investigating further. They learned that the owner of the mall lived out of state and would only consider selling at a very high price. The reality of the unattainable cost made those seeds planted in several hearts an unlikely vision, but still the idea would not let go.

When Beverly went on a trip to Haiti, she was surprised by a leader of a church there. He told her that the vision she had received previously was of God and would come true. *Sure*, she thought warily. Then he went on to describe the five pillars she dreamed of and the mall itself. There was no way he could have known this, and Beverly was stunned by what seemed like a divine affirmation. When she returned home from her travel, she told Ken about it, and he surprised her when he agreed it was time to start making this vision a reality. So Beverly's scratch paper became the blueprint of a plan.

As Beverly and Ken began meeting with people from the neighborhood around the mall, they discovered the neighbors who had been praying for the mall to be transformed. No wonder this vision had stayed on their minds. It seemed God was disrupting the hopelessness of this community with a tangible sign of God's presence moving anew into the neighborhood. Beverly likes to say that they started with "negative nothing," but no matter; they had a lot of prayer power!

Over the next few years, funding for the twenty million-dollar project came through some of the most miraculous and unexpected ways. R & R Marketplace bloomed out of seeds planted in prayer and persistence, thrown all over different kinds of soil with the expectation that God's work in their community was not finished yet—not by a long shot.

R & R Marketplace now offers early childhood education, addiction recovery support, workforce development, small business support, banking, a pharmacy, and continually evolving community resources. There's even a restaurant. And by the way, R & R Marketplace will also be the new, permanent home (in a building!) of the formerly nomadic Refuge and Restoration Church.

***

Imagine: Moises "Moy" Mendez's parents named him after Moses, the ultimate disruptor in the biblical story of Exodus. And Moy's personal journey movingly reflects Moses'. The Bible's Moses, as a member of a persecuted minority group, should never have grown to an adulthood with societal privileges bestowed on him; yet thanks to an innovative family, he became a leader in the very society that kept his people locked in systems of oppression.

After a childhood on the southside of Chicago in rough neighborhoods as a Mexican-American young man, Moy surprised himself when he was poised for success as a multi-degreed minister driving a sports car by age twenty-five. He served a wealthy congregation in the Chicago suburbs. The congregation where he worked then commissioned him to start a new church in Blue Island, where Moy grew up.

Very quickly, Moy realized that this impoverished community was not the same as his sending community and the approach he once used in ministry would not fit the new context in which he'd been called to serve. While his church started a food pantry, it felt woefully inadequate for the needs of the community. When the pandemic hit, the poverty and hopelessness of his neighbors became even more painfully impacting. His congregation began serving food to hungry neighbors, and before long they had served over ten thousand of their neighbors who were food insecure during the pandemic. Pastor Moy was stunned by the breadth of brokenness in his community.

Pastor Moy remembers that he would pray with people in need, but he yearned for solutions to accompany his prayers. He and his church's team of volunteers began looking for ways they could help people increase their personal agency. They felt called to disrupt the neighborhood's cycle of poverty with job training programs and meaningful support systems. They began by assessing what their unique contributions could be. They discovered their faith community had three skill sets they could share with others: auto mechanics, technology, and agriculture.

Unconventional though it was, the church began their step outside the box of traditional ministry. With a project to help people grow their own food, the Hope Center was born. Just a few years later, the Hope Center now offers a hydroponic community garden[1], a garage with an auto mechanics training program, and a technology service training center. The church's small congregation meets in and around all of these spaces.

Neighbors often come into the programs with no idea they are connecting to a faith-based organization. There's no preaching nor

[1] Hydroponics is a technique used to grow plants without soil using a nutrient-dense solution, which takes up much less space and 90 percent less water than traditional means of using soil.

requirements for the clients to profess a certain kind of faith. Even the volunteers are welcome no matter what they believe!

But people are often moved by the authenticity of the staff and the purpose of their work. One autistic young man spends time at the facility nearly every day. He took the brake certification class and passed it, giving him new confidence in himself. Now he is a mainstay volunteer.

Moy's dream is for the Hope Center to be replicated in other faith communities, addressing the needs in their neighborhoods with the resources available in their congregations, so that people can discover personal agency and not just a handout from their local church.

***

Imagine: Robert Rueda was walking with a student across the University of Texas Rio Grande Valley campus where he serves as the Baptist Student Ministries director. It was a chilly day, and Robert asked the student why he wasn't wearing a coat. The student hemmed and hawed about not usually needing one in the Rio Grande Valley with its normally warm temperatures. Robert chided him a little that he still needed a jacket, and the student finally admitted that not only did he not have a jacket, but he couldn't afford one. Robert says that moment changed his entire approach to student ministry.

Robert began to listen to students' experiences. He learned that many of the first-generation students he served grew up with nothing, working in fields with their parents. These students' enrollment in college was the result of an entire family's sacrifice and their shared hope for a better future.

In 2018, about the same time Robert started really listening to the stories of his students, the university completed a research project that revealed 48 percent of students at the campus were food insecure, meaning they did not always know how they would afford their next meal. Within eighteen months of that report, Robert and his student ministry partners had started Global Blends, a pay-what-you-can deli and coffee shop. Invested Faith was one of the first to invest in the Global Blends concept, giving them five thousand dollars to purchase a mobile coffee cart to enable them to increase business by working events and doing pop-up service. Everything took off from there. A local Baptist mission organization soon saw their powerfully effective ministry and gifted them a building to use.

At Global Blends, the food is top-notch and the coffee is excellent. Everyone is welcome to enjoy nourishment and time sitting around tables together, regardless of ability to pay. Instead of giving guests a bill for their order, the volunteers serving as baristas and wait staff simply ask, "What would you like to donate today?" During the pandemic they opened a drive-thru option and invited family members of students to eat with them as well. Now, seven years after it began, Global Blends has a volunteer student staff of twenty-seven and one full-time chef. Together they feed 1,200 students a month.

One of the earliest customers at Global Blends was a professor at the university. He ordered a coffee and donated five hundred dollars for it. When Robert followed up with him to ask why he had been so generous, the professor said, "I was once a student here, and I was often hungry. Then I had nowhere to go. I'm so grateful that students like I once was now have a place to go where they can be fed."

***

Imagine: Dr. Kit Evans-Ford leads Argrow's House, named after Kit's grandmother, who endured a lifetime of domestic violence. Even in the midst of experiencing such terror, Kit's grandmother Argrow was a kind and generous person who served as a deacon in the African Methodist Episcopal church where she belonged. Kit knew she wanted to serve other people like her grandmother someday. She became an AmeriCorps and Peace Corps volunteer as a young woman. During that time, Kit endured a violent assault herself. She searched tirelessly for a way to heal from that trauma and to come to terms with the long cycle of abuse in her family. Kit's determination to find wholeness in the midst of brokenness led her to seminary and to ongoing research on healing for traumatized women.

As Kit healed, she was determined to make her wellness count not only for herself, but for others. Though she eventually pursued ordination to ministry, Kit's first and continuing calling is to work outside of the walls of the church to use her gifts, skills, and experiences in imaginative ways to reach those who need God's love the most. Argrow's House was born out of Kit's own struggles, learning, and passion to use what she has been through to do good in the world.

Argrow's House, located in the Quad Cities Region of Davenport, Iowa, and Moline, Illinois, is a community of refuge for women in need of healing. Argrow's House offers free support services for women and their children recovering from domestic violence for as long as they need them. Along with a peaceful housing community, Argrow's House provides mental health counseling, art therapy, massage, and other services for survivors, including Saturday fun days for women and their children.

And that's just the beginning! Argrow's House is also a thriving social enterprise where women healing from violence are employed. They create beautiful bath and body products available in local gift shops and online. Residents also manage a lovely café in the Argrow's House gift shop. The business side of Argrow's House provides workplace skill development and a living wage for the women, as well as purposeful opportunities as they recover. You can palpably feel the disruption of violence by intentional rhythms of peaceful community at Argrow's House.

***

Imagine: Rev. Tamice Spencer-Helms' grandmother taught in the Baltimore public schools. Because of the excellence of her classroom, her grandmother was visited by Baltimore's mayor. He was so impressed with her teaching that he asked what he could do to help in her important work. Her answer was immediate and insistent: she asked for a washer and a dryer for her students so they could come to school in clean clothes. Tamice, as it turns out, is very much like her grandmother. When she began her ministry work as a university campus minister, Tamice noticed that the Black, first-generation college students she served were working with very little basic support to make them successful in their studies. They struggled with food insecurity and had little, if any, safety nets to catch them should a small or large setback come their way.

When Tamice found herself taking a very bright Black student to the train station to head home because she had run out of funds to pursue her dreams, Tamice was stopped in her tracks. She sensed the calling of God to clear the path for first-generation Black college students to thrive in their college years, not just survive if they were lucky. Sub:Culture was born. It began as an emergency fund for students so that minor challenges like car repairs didn't become a major block to their education. But it quickly blossomed into a structure of support for students. Once accepted into the program, a Sub:Culture fellow receives a $1,500 savings account, a small stipend, an academic success coach, and a "well of wisdom" mentor who serves as an encourager and adviser. In addition, students participate in weekly classes and retreats using the Soulful Leadership curriculum that Tamice created.

The goal of Sub:Culture is repair for Black college students and for our country. For Tamice, the financial help given to students can be thought of as reparations. People who want to invest in the holistic health of Black young adults can take monetary resources often accumulated over generations by ill-gotten gains and help to repair the historical wounds that still need healing. Sub:Culture now has fellows at six universities. Tamice believes creating a greenhouse for Black students helps them to name themselves against the status quo that would limit their lives. She proclaims in her daily work that supporting her students in substantive ways breaks generational cycles of poverty and brings life to the world.

Praise God for the way the Holy Spirit moves us out of our silos and weaves new networks of care! Because of the out-of-the-box ministry of these holy disruptors, first-generation college students have robust support as they build their futures, people living paycheck to paycheck are connected into a community that offers job skill development opportunities to secure their families' well-being, women escaping violence find a home and a springboard for new life, and an abandoned shopping mall connects people to their neighbors and the help they need. Imagine how you and your faith community could connect isolated people into new, compassionate communities that bring church to them.

A true revolution of values will soon cause us to question the fairness and justice of many of our past and present policies. On the one hand we are called to play the Good Samaritan on life's roadside, but that will be only an initial act. One day we must come to see that the whole Jericho Road must be transformed so that men and women will not be constantly beaten and robbed as they make their journey on life's highway. True compassion is more than flinging a coin to a beggar. It comes to see that an edifice which produces beggars needs restructuring.

—Martin Luther King Jr.[1]

[1] "Beyond Vietnam: Breaking the Silence," sermon delivered by Martin Luther King, Jr. at the Riverside Church in the City of New York, April 4, 1967.

CHAPTER 7

Disrupting Unjust Systems

How could people of faith become a force for not only helping others, but also for addressing unjust structures that cause our neighbors' suffering in the first place? Shouldn't our work as people of faith move beyond addressing painful wounds and delve into the unjust systems that result in these consequences?

Yes. The answer to that question is yes!

If you read the stories of Jesus carefully, you will see a fundamental conflict that runs as a theme through the gospel accounts of his life. From the very moment Jesus joined the crowds along the banks of the Jordan River and waded into the water to be baptized by his relative John, the people around him expected that his leadership would relieve them of the crippling domination of Roman rule. Jesus' neighbors were people who suffered tremendously from excessive taxation, unreasonable religious requirements, and a hand-to-mouth existence that negated their ability and stifled their creativity to work for change. Because of this systemic oppression, many of those who took note of the upstart rabbi assumed that he had arrived on the scene to orchestrate a major political overthrow. The truth was, of course, that the dismantling of systems Jesus came to teach was related less to government regimes and far more to revolutions of the heart.

Human history teaches us that kindness, justice, and fair treatment of our neighbors in need *never* organically emerge whenever vast systems of power hold sway in communities. Those systems, government or otherwise, are fueled by accumulation of power and resources. The hoarding of resources never ends in care for neighbors and certainly never in the dismantling of systems built for the very purpose of propping up systems of injustice.

Jesus, the consummate storyteller, spells this very pattern out in Luke's Gospel.[1] It's a story we hear infrequently read aloud, and there are compelling reasons to sweep it under the rug. In fact, Jesus told this story as crowds were gathering to hear him. They were trampling each other, the text says (with no absence of irony).

Here's how the story went. One of the crowd members who managed to push his way to the front, close enough for Jesus to hear him, yelled out: "Teacher! Tell my brother to share his inheritance with me!" To say this crowd member missed the point would be redundant, but Jesus answered, as he often did, with a story.

After a sharp word to his questioner about the danger of greed, Jesus told the story of a man whose crops had unexpectedly yielded a harvest far larger than he'd anticipated. Struck with the conundrum of what to do, the man decided to tear down the barns he had and build bigger and bigger barns, in which he could hold all the harvest his crops produced. The end result, the man reasoned, would be plenty of free time to relax, eat, drink, and be merry.

This solution seems to make a lot of sense to most of us, but not to Jesus. In the economy of Jesus, the principal goals of human effort are not to "eat, drink, and be merry."

Just think of all the other options that might have been available to that farmer: sharing his excess, offering his barns to a farmer with less, hiring workers at a fair wage to promote the local economy, giving some of his money away. The list goes on and on and proves the point with which Jesus ended that story: "Fool, tonight you will die. Now who will get the things you have prepared for yourself? This is the way it will be for those who hoard things for themselves and aren't rich toward God" (Luke 12:20–1).

This is precisely why anyone in search of power or wealth, domination or accumulation of assets, will read the story of Jesus with offense, or at least some confusion. What is it, exactly, that benefits

[1] See Luke 12:16–24.

me when I love my enemy, turn the other cheek, or give the coat off my back?[2]

Just like the political and social landscape surrounding Jesus' appearance on the scene, people of faith living in modern society also operate within systems built to make the rich richer. We too are part of systems that add to the crippling burden borne by those who have been told repeatedly to "pull themselves up by their bootstraps" but in fact don't possess even one decent pair of boots.

As it turns out, Jesus did not appear on earth with a plan for political domination and a command to hoard resources to protect ourselves. His message was unsettling, unpopular, and much more counterintuitive. *Give what you have away. Share with your neighbors. Stop along the side of the road to help someone who is vulnerable. Live your life with hands and hearts open, believing and living as if you know there is more than enough for everyone to thrive, if only we would turn our focus from ourselves to the good of the whole community around us.*

While all of the holy disruptors described in this book are building businesses and ministries that are pushing back at unjust systems, here you'll meet a few who have taken the challenge to *change* an unjust system seriously and in unique, innovative ways. Their work, like the work of Jesus, challenges the systems that keep us comfortable and restive in our self-righteous approaches to life. Their stories amplify the words of Jesus and the story he told about the farmer whose barns were bursting at the seams.

Just like the stories Jesus told, these stories should, at the very least, prick our consciences enough to make us look hard at our excess, *especially the excess of our faith institutions*, and ask what we have that might be used to challenge systems built to ensure that we're just fine while so many others do not have enough.

***

Imagine: The urgency of climate change does not appear on the agenda of most church board meetings. But Josh Richardson

---

[2] See Matthew 5:38–40.

wants it to be front and center as a matter of immediate concern for people of faith. Josh is an environmental scientist and a public theologian. His calling to connect pastoring with care for the planet came when he nearly lost his life to cancer. Results of his treatment left him permanently disabled and with a choice to make. Like the reminder Jesus gave the excessively wealthy farmer, Josh learned in a painful and clarifying way that he was not going to live forever, a fact of which he thinks most humans are not adequately aware. Josh prayerfully wondered: How could he most effectively spend the time he has been given to live?

This serious personal health crisis catapulted pastor/scientist Josh to make a radical life decision. He quit his job as a wetlands geologist for a state geological survey, and he started Brugmansia Ministries,[3] a nonprofit that helps churches prepare to be useful for God's healing of the world in the midst of climate change and its resultant migration.[4] Josh believes that ministry is resilience and, since the crisis of climate change is now at our doorsteps, the time for churches to pay attention to it is now. The congregation Josh leads in St. Louis has become an emergency shelter, which can be used during a migration displacement crisis. They are also working to become an urban food hub with outdoor permaculture, conventional agriculture, and indoor hydroponics and aquaponics, illustrating the ministry of resilient preparation for other faith communities ready to address the realities of climate change.

Pastor Josh's goal is not to replicate that in every church building in the world. Instead, his focus is to help congregations assess their

[3] "Brugmansia" is a genus of flowering plants that are commonly called angel's-trumpets. The name, Brugmansia Ministries, references the organization's focus on combining scientific and religious knowledge to call forth a new vision for how religious communities can more justly serve our world as we struggle with climate change and climate-induced migration.

[4] Climate-change-caused migration, or climate migration, refers to the movement of people due to the impacts of climate change, including both sudden events like floods and droughts, and slower-moving changes like sea level rise and water stress. This form of migration is increasing as the effects of climate change become more severe, impacting livelihoods, forcing people to relocate, and potentially leading to cross-border movements.

unique contexts. He wants faith communities to become partners with and supporters of their neighbors in forward-thinking ways. He thinks congregations can change the baseline conditions many people tolerate and propel their communities to thrive, whatever the future holds.

For example, a small congregation in Georgia is in the process of becoming a resiliency center for its community because of Brugmansia. The church building is in decline, as is the congregation in member participation and financial strength. They invited Pastor Josh to talk about climate resilience and to present an idea of how they could use their resources, which primarily are their building and the farmland around it. Together, they identified that they already have all the existing infrastructure to produce food and provide clean water for their community. They also have plenty of space for green energy production and low-income housing on the site.

In conversation with a potential partner for this project, a funder offered to underwrite those costs in exchange for office space in the building and the standing invitation to show other churches the facilities as an example of what is possible. Now that church is moving toward a ministry that is truly transformational. They have an urgency to do the best they can with what they have to change their community's resilience in natural disasters. Churches don't live forever either, but their legacies can.

***

Imagine: Marisa L.R. Prince and Calvin D. Lee met in 2018 while working for a Massachusetts Senate campaign. Though the candidate didn't survive the primary, Marisa and Calvin discovered that they still felt a calling to tackle polarization and bridge divides. Committed to seeking guidance from God for next steps, Marisa and Calvin prayed and fasted for five days, meeting daily to piece together strategy and ideas. At the end of that week, they launched [GOSPEL], an initiative creating content and spaces to challenge the Church to reimagine identity and engagement with the world, piloted by a project called American Awakening.

American Awakening unleashed a full slate of creative vehicles raging against the divisiveness of the 2020 election cycle and calling people to form authentic community, funded by their cross-discipline partnerships. The campaign networked with organizations including the National Association of Evangelicals, William Morris Endeavor, Relevant Media Group, Christianity Today, and Q Ideas to write and produce critical efforts counterprogramming against polarization of the country. The American Awakening projects included a global concert event featuring well-known contemporary Christian music artists, a book with a foreword by David Brooks[5], newspaper articles, a seventy-one-episode podcast/livestream, docuseries episodes, and national thought leader gatherings.

At the end of 2020, Marisa and Calvin followed the leading of the Holy Spirit toward something they call "radical togetherness." Since then, they've produced films like *Are We There YET,* about American Christian nationalism and the Church's responsibility to repair, and *SUNDAY DINNER*, examining attitudes about Christian gun consumption in the wake of the Covenant School shooting. They are also building spaces for education and community organizing, like *[GOSPEL] Minneapolis*, a livestream special featuring local activists and faith leaders responding to the murder of George Floyd, and the *Boston Activation Experience*, which brought their community together to develop new strategies for addressing Christian nationalism on the anniversary of January 6, 2021. Together, they're pushing for the Church to disrupt inequity and disavow empire, instead championing liberation for all in the name of Jesus. They are reaching people who have left the Church, or never even tried it, on the screens and in the streets across the country.

***

Imagine: Leslee Matthews was a precocious kid who called a family meeting when she was ten years old. She announced to her parents, who were both ministers, that her vocational plan was to be a lawyer who helps women and children. Leslee's calling became even

[5] The book is: John Kingston, *American Awakening: Eight Principles to Restore the Soul of America* (Zondervan, 2020).

more urgent and clear in college when her best friend was murdered by her husband.

Leslee eventually became both an attorney and a social worker, specializing in family violence. When she saw the gaping need for accessible, affordable legal services for victims of abuse, Leslee founded Speak Out and Up Law (SOUL) in her native Hawaii. SOUL provides pro bono and "low bono" legal services to women and girls who have experienced discrimination and violence. Their clients have had cases argued all the way to the state Supreme Court on behalf of women who need a voice.

Proverbs 31:8–9 is their vision and prayer: "Speak out on behalf of the voiceless, and for the rights of all who are vulnerable. Speak out in order to judge with righteousness and to defend the needy and the poor."

Leslee's goal is to end domestic violence in her lifetime.

All of this powerful advocacy is done in partnership with Leslee's home congregation. Living Way Church Maui calls themselves a "faith-based community resource." Imagine *that*! They are an around-the-clock center for caring for their neighbors, especially after the 2024 Maui wildfires. When the needs of SOUL's clients are complex, Leslee connects them with the resources of food, transportation, and community support her congregation offers. The church supports SOUL's regular workshops like "Knowing Your Rights" and hosts Indigenous people's empowerment conferences. Together SOUL and Living Way are changing the world for women, girls, and people in need in Hawaii.

***

Imagine: Pastor Stephen "Cue" Jn-Marie was a successful rapper signed to a major record label. After performing in front of a crowd of sixty-five thousand people, he realized that even though he felt a rush every time he performed, immediately afterward he felt empty. He wondered how big the next crowd needed to be for him to feel the rush again. Recognizing the danger of that trend, Pastor Cue knelt and prayed: *God, don't let me lose my soul to this.*

Soon after, Pastor Cue saw the movie *Malcom X* and felt like he heard God's voice saying to him, "He died too soon. I want you to do what he did." At the time Pastor Cue was not a churchgoer, but when a friend invited him, he went. That day, the preacher's sermon title was "He Died Too Soon." Pastor Cue heard a calling that he has pursued ever since.

Pastor Cue now pastors a "church without walls" called The Row on Skid Row in Los Angeles, one of the poorest areas in the United States. Cue's influence extends further in his work as an activist with Clergy and Laity United for Economic Justice, an organization that equips faith-rooted leaders to advocate for marginalized people in their communities. He also operates a nonprofit organization called "Creating Justice LA," which birthed the Hip Hop Smoothie Shop, a worker-owned cooperative where wages start at twenty dollars per hour. The Hip Hop Smoothie Shop currently employs fifteen people at a living wage. The shop regularly holds community potlucks and concerts for free.

Services for The Row are held on Friday nights, and Pastor Cue constantly tells the volunteers from his church at these events *not* to invite folks to come to worship with them. He wants people to feel free to participate without a sense of obligation. But people come to worship anyway, following the pastor and church leaders by showing up at church, too. They sense the authentic community-building and want to be a part of it. All kinds of people, wanting better for themselves and their neighbors, join in prayer and service through The Row. And now the entire Skid Row neighborhood has become Pastor Cue's parish, building a community that disrupts a system built to function as a cradle-to-prison pipeline.

***

Imagine: Pastor Chris Lawrence lives in East Harlem. He and his family, including four kids and a large dog, have moved seven times in ten years in part because of the gentrification and rising rent of their neighborhoods. Almost all of the young people in whom the communities invest have to move elsewhere as they become adults because they can't afford to live in their home neighborhoods.

That migration creates a "brain drain" for important neighborhood-based occupations like teachers and social workers. It also means the pews of East Harlem faith communities are mostly filled with elderly folks and a few commuters who used to live in the neighborhood and now travel back in to attend worship services. Meanwhile, East Harlem residents are working hard at two to three jobs in order to afford their rent.

Because of this structurally unjust situation, many who live in the neighborhood have no time for church, much less for getting to know their neighbors. The result? A stark vacuum of neighborliness. There is no one to smile at the mail carrier or check in on the elderly couple living across the street. No neighbors to watch out for your place when you travel. No friends to casually invite to dinner.

Originally from London, Chris participated in a housing ministry there that operated three hundred houses for the purpose of giving residents a break from price gouging that occurs in big cities. He began to wonder if something similar could happen in East Harlem. And El Barrio Homes was born.

El Barrio Homes is an "urban village" concept that revolves around a shared condominium building where those in occupations such as teaching and social work can live at an affordable rate. Local congregations support the work by investing in the project and engaging residents to build community. Investors from the neighborhood and beyond sign on for seven years then receive a return on their investment, or they can "re-up" and keep supporting the work.

Residents' rent can be adjusted on a sliding scale basis, depending on how much time they have available to volunteer in service to their neighbors through churches and other nonprofit organizations. This "hyper-local" approach helps church members who commute to engage with their church's neighborhoods, foster the interest of neighbors to seek each other out, and care about one another. El Barrio Homes is disrupting the greed of the housing market with an infusion of neighborliness fueled by savvy strategy.

Hallelujah for vision to see how faith in action can truly change the world! Imagine that you and your faith community might become a force for not only helping people, but also changing unjust systems that cause people to need help in the first place. Amidst questions of the church's survival, we must not miss the essential question: Where is your congregation called to invest its spiritual and financial wealth in order to set its neighbors free?

Look, the world is always ending somewhere.
Somewhere the sun has come crashing down.
Somewhere it has gone completely dark.
Somewhere it has ended with the gun, the knife, the fist.
Somewhere it has ended with the slammed door, the shattered hope.
Somewhere it has ended with the utter quiet that follows the news from the phone, the television, the hospital room.
Somewhere it has ended with a tenderness that will break your heart.
But, listen, this blessing means to be anything but morose. It has not come to cause despair.
It is simply here because there is nothing a blessing is better suited for than an ending,
nothing that cries out more for a blessing than when a world is falling apart.
This blessing will not fix you, will not mend you, will not give you false comfort; it will not talk to you about one door opening when another one closes.
It will simply sit itself beside you among the shards and gently turn your face toward the direction from which the light will come, gathering itself about you as the world begins again.

—Jan Richardson[1]

[1] Jan Richardson, "Blessing When the World Is Ending," *The Painted Prayer Book*, July 18, 2016, https://paintedprayerbook.com/2016/07/18/blessing-when-the-world-is-ending/. Reprinted with permission from Jan Richardson.

CHAPTER 8

How Is This Church?

For decades, religious leaders have been plied with resources promising to stem the tide of institutional decline. From "use this five-step plan to create committed leaders who attend, tithe, and depend on their congregation for the health of their families" to "implement this failsafe method for church growth: coffee bar in the narthex, drums in the auditorium, and small groups in every neighborhood," faith communities desperate for help have no end to people glad to try. Usually for a steep price!

Occasionally these strategies work, of course, but they seem to prey on the assumption that if the church is losing health—if the institution declines or even fails—so goes the message it claims to represent: a message of Jesus' continuing transformational work in the world. This assumption, adopted by a plethora of congregations and their leaders over the course of multiple decades, is deeply flawed. Why? Because many of these five-steps-to-success approaches negate the underlying and fundamental truth that the work of God does not depend on the flourishing or *even the existence* of the institutions we have built to house our best attempts to live out the message of Jesus.

There's nothing wrong with a healthy church, of course! Where we get into trouble is when our efforts, our resources, and our faith are bound up in an institution. Because the Church, after all, is not God.

Here's some good news as we face the reality of institutional decline: When we don't have an easy plan for church growth, when we don't know where to turn for answers, when we can't find any clarity about the future of a religious institution we love, we can always come back to Jesus. Jesus entered our world with no institutional endorsement. He was born into the minority religion of Judaism, a people who suffered excruciatingly under imperial domination and whose temple was crushed while Jesus' stories were being recorded for the first time. And his aim was to teach us a new way to live; he never set out to found a new religion or to build another institution.

Every instructional story we read about the life and ministry of Jesus required no ordination credentials, no Book of Order, no liturgical ritual. His message functioned independently of any insulating protection from the harsh realities of Roman rule all around him or even temple protocol. And in response to Jesus' life, his disciples wrote down every gospel story in the face of political disruption, horrific violence, and varied resistances to the Roman Empire, offering those stories as a beacon of light for a new path.

With his actions and teachings, Jesus proclaimed the reign of another power entirely: the Kingdom of God. Working sometimes within *and often outside* the structures of the religious institution into which he was born, Jesus did not dismiss nor disdain the traditions that had formed him. Instead, he kept beckoning those entrenched in institutions to do something they were unaccustomed to doing. He asked them to pivot with the lively wind of God's Spirit, to change, to evolve, to become what God is always in the process of creating—something new. Something that gives the world a glimpse of the ultimately victorious and always renewing power of self-giving love.

Jesus did this by nurturing communities that included, embraced, and even empowered those who fell through the cracks of social and religious networks—foreigners, widows, children, differently-abled people struggling to survive in a society never meant to make room for them. And though the time he spent teaching and living this radical approach to faith community was very limited, Jesus worked hard to prepare his friends to teach others so they would keep on with the work he'd begun to preach good news to the poor, release to the captives, recover sight for the blind, and liberate the oppressed.[1]

[1] See Acts 1:8; Luke 4:17–18.

Jesus' early followers, empowered by the Holy Spirit to gather courage to continue the mandate he'd given them, convened in homes while sharing food with anyone in need and "demonstrating God's goodness to everyone." They "devoted themselves to the apostles' teaching, to the community, to their shared meals, and to their prayers" (Acts 2:42–47).

It is sometimes said that Jesus came to bring the reign of God to earth and our best attempts to live that out became what we now know as the church. Over the changes of two millennia, a church in the United States often looks like a far cry from fishing together, having a picnic on a Galilean hillside, or meeting in homes and sharing food among outcasts no one else would ever willingly invite to their table. Sometimes we too easily forget that pews and pulpits haven't always been what it takes to be a community gathered in Jesus' name. And now that we can see traditional churches closing their doors all around us, it is time to remember what the scenes of faith communities at work looked like in the New Testament.

Research confirms that the American church's reputation for helping others is waning with both the general public and in the perception even of active church participants. We are not, in other words, known for the very work that birthed us: the pursuit of justice and the healing of the world.[2] We've become accustomed to *talking* about opening the eyes of the blind, but when a church opens an eye clinic, it seems odd. We preach about setting people free from oppression, yet a congregation becoming a non-predatory lending agency doesn't fit our definition of church. We say all people are welcome at the table of our Lord, but too many of our church kitchens remain empty to those longing for basic nourishment all week long.

Rev. Teresa Hord Owens, general minister and president of the Christian Church (Disciples of Christ), often repeats her mantra for the church: "We must become the church we say we are."[3] Are we

---

[2] "18–35-Year-Olds Rate the Church's Reputation for Justice," Barna, December 4, 2019, https://www.barna.com/research/churchs-reputation-for-justice/.

[3] "Office of the General Minister and President," Christian Church (Disciples of Christ) in the United States and Canada, September 8, 2023, https://disciples.org/uncategorized/office-of-the-general-minister-and-president.

ready to break out of our limited understanding of what church is to really live into expressions of faith that look and feel radically different from what we are comfortable with? We believe that can happen, that it must happen, and the good news is that recent research suggests that a majority of American Christians are ready to help the church refocus on what is truly impactful for their neighbors.[4]

Though church can and does happen in cathedrals, we know from the earliest examples—and most convincingly from the actions of Jesus—that church can happen anywhere. For at least two hundred years, the first followers of Jesus met in homes to be church together. And though thoughtful architecture can undoubtedly positively shape a community, a beautiful church building is not essential to creating or sustaining a faith community.

What constitutes a Christian faith community then?

Traditional Protestant Christian denominations have determined that a church exists wherever word (the proclamation of scripture) and sacrament (the rituals like baptism and communion) are practiced in community. Is this a robust enough understanding of church? Robert Rueda tells students who volunteer at the pay-what-you-can Global Blends restaurant that church doesn't look like going to Sunday school or sitting in a pew. He teaches them that church looks like serving alongside other believers, using our abilities and time to show God's love to those who need to see it in tangible ways. Church happens, he says, out of organic relationships formed over time *by caring for people in need* together. For Marisa Prince and Calvin Lee, church is communal seeking, worshiping, building, and growing. Though connected to a traditional church, they've experienced true faith community most notably in their organizational work with [GOSPEL] across the country. Praying, fasting, studying scripture, and serving with their gifts are all key elements of the work and powerfully inspired by the Holy Spirit.

What makes a church a church? According to the descriptions in the book of Acts[5], the first "community of believers" gathered for

[4] "Christians Want to Help the Church Realign to 'Be What Jesus Intended,'" Barna, October 23, 2024, https://www.barna.com/trends/church-priorities/.

[5] See Acts 2:42–47; Acts 4:32–25.

worship, preaching, teaching, sharing with those in need, fellowship, and evangelism, or sharing the good news with everyone.[6] Let's use these purposes, or actions, of the church to reflect on the stories you've read.

Do you see *worship* in these stories? Where do you recognize the praise and enjoyment of God?

We think of the Living Water Community Center, which worships on Sunday mornings as a traditional congregation, yet throughout the week, daily, offers a rhythm for pilgrims to observe while keeping bees, tending the garden, and sharing contemplative practices whether they visit for a day or live there full time. We reflect on the Hip Hop Smoothie Shop, where people earn a living wage and experience the genuine presence of God over community potlucks and concerts so winsomely that they are drawn into more worship at The Row church, where the potluck volunteers came from, on Sunday mornings. Not to mention Urban Roots Farm, where people step into nature's sanctuary while serving and enjoying the creation of God together.

What about *preaching*? How are these innovators proclaiming the reign of God coming in Christ, engaging the scriptures of our faith, and changing the lives of their hearers?

We think of the Hope Center, where budding mechanics are learning their trade amidst the encouragement of volunteers and staff who are authentically sharing God's love for each person as they embody the good news coming into their lives. And consider the challenging work of the Rhode Island Community Investment Cooperative calling to us all, investors and entrepreneurs, with the challenge and charge of reflecting on how our spiritual values align with our financial practices. Or the way Brugmansia is challenging business as usual by urging our churches to take scripture in one hand and the daily news in the other—and, for the love of God, do something to prepare for climate change.

Where is *teaching* happening in these nontraditional spaces? How is this work passing on a faith that develops holy disruptors in the way of Jesus?

---

[6] Thank you to Rev. Dr. Katie Hays and her work with the Disciples of Christ North Texas Area New Church Ministry for these insights.

Think about the Inheritance Theater Project, where community members wrestle for weeks with sacred texts to create a play to share with the community, often in sanctuaries. And consider the Speak Out and Up Law Firm as they work within their community to educate people on their rights and worth as children of God. Reflect on Deep Time's opportunities for mentoring and learning during weekly groups at the county jail and in recovery support programs, not to mention the day-to-day discipleship training for returning citizens working at Deep Time.

Sharing with those in need is another mark of the church from the book of Acts. How are these communities useful to their neighbors in self-sacrificing ways?

Consider Village Green RVA, offering wrap-around care to anyone who needs it, coordinating dozens of partners to make sure everyone who walks in their doors is seen and served. And we think of the ministry of Argrow's House, coming alongside women recovering from violence, giving them peace and holding space for their healing with housing and counseling services. Also remember the work of Sub:Culture and Global Blends Coffee Shop, serving historically marginalized college students so that they are empowered to serve others. Jesus called this "welcoming the Kingdom of God," living our faith out loud so that others can see it and join in. But also, and perhaps most especially, Jesus hoped that our faith would have hands and feet in the world, making substantive impact that will move us, if incrementally, toward the dream God has for the world.

And *fellowship*, perhaps one of the most healing parts of faith community, shows up all over the stories of these social entrepreneurs! How do these organizations build authentic communities and growing friendships?

We think of El Barrio Homes, working to allow people to stay in their neighborhoods to get to know one another. They are establishing a caring partnership with their building mates by connecting them to volunteer each week to help defray their rent expenses and make sustainable connections with neighbors. And imagine the four-church-strong WKC, with its waiting list of food trucks wanting to use church kitchens, hosting gourmet feasts and offering pastoral care to culinary entrepreneurs while church members purchase their food. Think of the women living at Argrow's House, working alongside each other on their own healing, creating beautiful products together to support themselves, doing life together.

Where do you see *sharing the gospel*, the good news, with everyone? How do these communities invite and engage people who don't know the hope of Christ or the power of a healthy faith community?

We think of the work of R & R Marketplace, giving a tangible and very visible example of God's incarnation among us by turning abandoned buildings into a vibrant community hub. Now people who were once without help pour into that building to receive all kinds of services and empowerment, all within Refuge and Restoration Church's shepherding care. Also, reflect on Forai's ministry of connecting refugee women with a support network and job skills training, all while gently proclaiming the love of God in Jesus Christ with those who are curious to hear about it. Imagine the work of [GOSPEL] as they create films, concerts, and other media projects to spread the message that following Jesus doesn't mean being a Christian nationalist. Talk about sharing the good news!

Which of the stories you've read here do *you* think express authentic faith community in new places? We are calling on people of faith in this moment of holy disruption to expand our theological vision of what a church can be. We believe that communities of people working to heal the world together are, in fact, more similar to what Jesus did during his time on earth than even traditional stained-glass windows and formal liturgy. In his commentary on Matthew's gospel, biblical scholar Warren Carter writes:

> At least since the Reformation, the marks of the one, holy, apostolic, and catholic church have comprised word (preaching) and sacrament (baptism, Eucharist). But here the marks of the church comprise mission, powerlessness, vulnerability, poverty, suffering. For Matthew, the church is about actions consistent with the mission and qualities of Jesus.

> . . In societies where creature comforts, wealth, security, power, and status are so important, (Matthew) offers the massive challenge for churches to be always moving obediently to embrace active, countercultural mission for others.[7]

Furthermore, and this is understandably fear-filled for some, the theology undergirding our thought here is a strong conviction that *the work of God that heals the world very often shows up in ways we would least expect.* After all, according to the apostle Paul, "there are *different* spiritual gifts but the same Spirit; and there are *different* ministries and the same Lord; and there are *different* activities but the same God who produces all of them in everyone" (1 Corinthians 12:4–6, emphasis added). For us to faithfully represent the way of Jesus, we have to cast the net wide to harness all the *different* possibilities and partners we can find to do the work of repairing the world.

But is our own faith diminished when we join the work of people of other faiths, or people of no faith at all, or of people who worship very differently from us?

If we look to the example of Jesus, the resounding answer to that question is no, not in the least! Like the Gentile magi who came to acknowledge the Christ child then returned to their own country in Matthew's chapter 2, and the Syrophoenician woman who bantered with Jesus for the healing of her child in both Matthew and Mark's gospels, we welcome the surprising connections the Holy One makes between people whose hearts are joined for the sake of the healing of the world. Can an urban farm in downtown St. Louis hold the seeds of a faith community? We say yes. Even if the people who run it aren't ministers and don't hold formal services?

We say yes.

***

Asking these questions about what constitutes a church while considering a new path, maybe even holy disruption, in your

[7] Warren Carter, *Matthew: Storyteller, Interpreter, Evangelist* (Ada, Michigan: Baker Press, 2004), 84.

community of faith will be influenced by the denominational polity that governs your congregation. Most denominations are now beginning to pay attention to the serious decline in which many congregations find themselves. However, the problem we currently face within the denominational/congregational relationship dynamic is the plain truth that denominations are in decline right along with the churches they serve. This adds a complication to this moment: Who survives? Who gets to say where the resources go? Are we spending our time competing with each other rather than freeing each other to dream about holy disruption?

These are nuanced questions with variety depending upon the denomination(s) to which your congregation belongs, if any. Their answers are not easy to discuss or to define; in many cases, there are also considerable legal issues at play. Navigating this moment with the mandate of Jesus at the heart of our work is critically important because money, power, land, and resources have the potential to bring out the basest human behavior.

Those holding considerable wealth and using it for the purpose of preserving our denominational institutions must be invited into the terrifically scary and potentially transformational work that they have the ability and resources to fund in world-changing ways. We must have denominational leaders equally as willing to take risks as the holy disruptors in these pages. We pray that church judicatory staff members understand that the work of God will not and cannot stay contained within institutions. We pray they will have the courage to lead us to radically embrace a theology of abundance that will free congregations to follow the movement of God's Spirit.

Resources in vast quantities are held in denominational entities of many different expressions. Our dream is for these resources to be used in ways that risk the abundant and unexpected blossoming of something new. Our denominational leaders might be tempted to hang on to traditional and comfortable institutional vehicles holding resources that might instead seed the future. Leaders with power to withhold or deploy resources held in denominational storehouses must now be challenged, too, to use what has been held for a rainy day to plant the seeds that the rain will nurture. Because it is indeed currently raining.

It is not uncommon for holy disruptors to face incredulous responses to suggestions that risk the use of denominational resources to try something new. Instead of hearing "I can't propose ideas like this! I have a board I have to answer to! We have rules to follow," we hope for them to hear "Tell me more. We need to learn from you. How can we support your ministry?" We call on denominational leaders to do just that. Lead us. Show us how to risk something big for something good.[8] Fuel and fund the new thing; see what God will do! We invite you to make holy disruption your own spiritual practice. Maybe in every meeting you can, very boldly, ask, "How are we seeding the future of faith communities with all that we have?"

But at the very least, don't discourage people willing to risk everything to follow the wind of the Spirit. God's work does not stop in this world until all things are made new![9] How sad it would be to miss the wild and wonderful disruption of God's Spirit while carefully guarding traditions and endowments and, in the process, completely be left out of the new thing that God is creating.

During the nineteenth century, religious denominations built significant and creative organizations for the purpose of social benefit. Now, however, many religious institutions are unwilling to tolerate the risks necessary for entrepreneurship and innovation. This matters, not only because our denominations have a compelling moral vision for the good that can be done in the world, but also because of the tremendous capital our institutions still hold. Instead of being bold and courageous with these tremendous resources—moral as well as financial—too many Christians are preoccupied with a narrative of scarcity and holding on to what we have as best we can.[10]

---

[8] A partial paraphrase of words offered by the Reverend William Sloane Coffin as his signature benediction while serving as senior pastor at The Riverside Church in the City of New York.

[9] See Revelation 21:5.

[10] Amy K. Butler, "Vision," Invested Faith, https://www.investedfaith.org/vision.

We need denominations, seminaries, and other church institutions to serve congregations first and invest in congregations again, instead of the other way around. Our congregations are not made to support denominations; our denominations are made to support our congregations! We need our institutions to *disrupt themselves* by encouraging innovative leaders, both clergy and lay, with their substantial resources. Respectfully, we ask: How much bigger do our endowments need to be if there are very few churches for our denominations to support any more?

If our true aim is to be a movement for healing in our broken world[11], we may have to consider that using our resources to prop up familiar institutions and traditional programming we've engaged for decades may not be the most effective approach to finding the next expression of gospel work in the world. It is so very threatening even to suggest a shift like this. It is not safe, it does not guarantee measured outcomes, and it might be a risk too high for many of us to take.

But some are taking it! The Christian Church (Disciples of Christ) in the Southwest Region recently offered grants of up to forty thousand dollars for innovative ministry projects. After assessing the accumulated yield from their long-term investments over the last few years, these regional denominational leaders prayerfully discerned that reinvesting that money in their institutions was not the most faithful thing they could do. The most faithful thing they could imagine to do with that abundant money was to invest it in faith communities exercising bold faith in innovative ways. The grants are for congregations doing "out of the box" ministry, moving beyond charity to empowering their neighbors and igniting long-term change. They know that while adding money to ideas doesn't mean success, it can be fuel for fresh expressions of faith and community that grow into sustainable, impactful, world-changing work.

Certainly, investing in new and untested ventures will sometimes result in failure—something Jesus himself experienced. But recall that Jesus and the friends he taught changed the world. What might

[11] Or, as the Christian Church (Disciples of Christ) proclaims as its motto, "a movement for wholeness in a fragmented world."

happen if one or two little seeds are planted? What if they take root and grow, even in unconventional ways? And what if they accomplish some measure of repair in a world so desperately broken? What if?

In his December 21, 2024, *New York Times* op-ed, Ross Douthat, a Roman Catholic, expressed cautious optimism regarding signs that some Americans may be reconnecting with religion, but outside traditional contexts. Says Douthat: "There is statistical evidence that the latest wave of secularization has reached some sort of limit. There is suggestive cultural evidence that secular liberalism has lost faith in itself, that many people miss not just religion's moral vision but also its metaphysical horizons, that the arguments for religious belief might be getting a new hearing."

He adds: "But different probably means really different, not just a return to what existed in the past. The last bastions of the before times, the old religious establishments, are likely to remain in existential trouble. For instance … the Protestant Mainline isn't about to leap up from its sickbed. Likewise, groups such as the Southern Baptists and the Mormons, fast growing a few decades ago and struggling today, aren't going to automatically rebound or boom again." He concludes: "Instead, any growth is likely to be nondenominational, subcultural, mystical and *sui generis*, with notable flowerings in places where traditional faith has rarely grown before."[12]

Pastor Amy founded Invested Faith to identify, resource, and connect those who are doing just this: creating "church" in unconventional places and unconventional ways, pushing us traditional church people to stretch our imaginations about how church happens and where and in what ways we can show up to support it. Many of the funds Invested Faith channels to new and innovative ideas have come from traditional churches who reached completion[13] but who long for a legacy that lives beyond their institutional life.

[12] Ross Douthat, "Religion Is in Decline. This Christmas Seems Different," *New York Times,* December 21, 2024, https://www.nytimes.com/2024/12/21/opinion/religion-christmas-revival.html.

[13] "Completion" is a term we have learned recently from pastors working to help churches discern if they have come to the end of their day-to-day mission together. The word is used intentionally instead of "closure."

Invested Faith is always searching for faith-rooted entrepreneurs, many of whom you've met in these pages, who are creating new economic models (businesses) that are changing unjust systems. We believe this is one powerful area where a new expression of church is emerging. Our goal is to help those of us in traditional church spaces, distracted by decline and fear, to find the courage to use our assets to come alongside Invested Faith Fellows and other holy disruptors. We want to strengthen and follow the lead of those who have somehow found the courage to step out, to try something new, and to believe with their whole lives that God's Spirit is ever and always on the move, cajoling us to come out of safe places into places of possibility.

A faithful preacher will remind us that if we read just past our favorite "glory in the highest" passages describing the birth of Jesus in the second chapter of Luke, we learn that he eventually returned to his hometown, Nazareth. There, Jesus invited the people he'd known his whole life to join him in a totally new way of understanding God's work in the world. When Jesus began his work, chapter 4 of the Gospel of Luke says, he entered the synagogue and read from the prophet Isaiah:

"The Spirit of the Lord is upon me,
because the Lord has anointed me.
He has sent me to teach good news to the poor,
to proclaim release for the prisoners
and recovery of sight to the blind,
to liberate the oppressed,
and to proclaim the year of the Lord's favor." (Luke 4:18–19)

Then Jesus sat down and declared that this scripture (Isaiah 61:1–3) had been fulfilled in his coming.[14]

Again, which of the stories you've read here do you think especially expresses authentic faith community in new places? Maybe not all of them seem like "church" to you; maybe they seem like good community outreach ministry, but not church.

---

[14] See Luke 4:20.

Maybe whether efforts of goodness and healing can be called "church" is not even the right question.

Maybe a better question than defining what a church is or is not might be: Would Jesus recognize these innovative ministries as his own?

If so, let us pay attention.

i hope i die

warmed

by the life that i tried

to live

—Nikki Giovanni[1]

[1] Nikki Giovanni, "The Life I Led," *The Collected Poetry 1968–1998* (New York: William Morrow, 2007), 203.

CHAPTER 9

A Theology of Hope

Hope fuels our imagination for the future of faith communities in the United States. And hope begins with our eschatology, which is our belief about what happens in the End, with a capital E, when all is said and done. If we embrace an eschatology that tenaciously clings to hope and refuses to cede to despair, we become people of faith poised for the future God has always imagined for us and for our world.

But it's not easy to make our way to an eschatology of hope.

Thanks to the wildly popular *Left Behind* novels that hit the shelves in the mid-1990s and continued churning out a this-world-is-going-to-hell-in-a-handbasket kind of theology for well over a decade, many American Christians adopted an eschatology fueled by fear instead of hope. In other words, we've been socially conditioned not by holy texts, mind you, but by popular fiction, that one day God will "rapture" true believers up out of earth and whisk us away to another place where we can leave this broken world behind: if we have prayed the right prayers and attended the approved churches, we will be headed away from destruction, leaving the planet and all other people behind to face their inevitable end.

Adopting this kind of eschatology, either intentionally taught or by osmosis through the influence of mass-produced fiction, has had devastating effects on the life and witness of faith communities. Many people of faith in our country have adopted an eschatology in which the current world doesn't matter. They believe it's going to hell anyway and Christians have the golden ticket out.

When this is the eschatological underpinning of our worldview, then our time, energy, effort, and resources will be spent on pulling believers out of the world as often as possible, keeping them in standard worship styles in familiar sanctuaries, and giving them the peace and strength they need to endure until the day of our rescue. Ardent communities of this nature will work with sincere intention to "seek out the lost" and bolster their ranks before the day of doom.[1]

On the other hand, if we believe that with the coming of Jesus, God gave birth to a new creation right here on earth, both in and among us, and that this planet will remain in the care of God come what may, then we have purposeful work to do here and now in repairing the world.

Every Sunday, most Christians recite the Lord's Prayer, a prayer Jesus taught his disciples. It contains perhaps one of the simplest, most beautiful expressions of a wholly different kind of eschatology than the one we learned from all those *Left Behind* books. This is the eschatology that Jesus came to teach us and show us: "Our Father in heaven, hallowed be your name. Your kingdom come. Your will be done, *on earth as it is in heaven*" (Matthew 6:9–10 NRSV, emphasis added). This prayer articulates with crystal clarity an eschatology distinctly different from inevitable doom and destruction. Instead, this prayer tells us that God is bringing heaven here.

If Christians claim to follow Jesus, and even pray the prayer he taught his disciples to pray, then there is no golden ticket off a burning planet. There is instead a powerful, holy, and urgent mandate to do exactly what Jesus did—believe and behave as if heaven is indeed currently and eventually coming to earth as God's will is done here.

Listen to our Jewish friends who teach us of *tikkun olam*, our holy command to repair the world. This is the eschatology by which Jesus was formed. This was the call to his disciples when he taught them to pray "your kingdom come, on earth as it is in heaven."

[1] For more insights on the effect of our beliefs about the End on how we act in the world, see the work of Robin G. Veldman in *The Gospel of Climate Skepticism: Why Evangelical Christians Oppose Action on Climate Change* (University of California Press, 2019).

Rejecting the idea that the world is headed for destruction, our job as people and communities of faith becomes uniquely distinct from the fire-and-brimstone fearmongering that *Left Behind* preachers would like us to assume. Instead, we are called to live as people who know the inbreaking of God *is already here on earth*, and we are to be it, to find it, and to put all the energy of our faith-fueled conviction to work within it.

To that end, we are to be people who live insisting that God is already here among us, that God's reign is at hand, and that we are harbingers of heaven right here. And if, as many of us pray each Sunday in worship, God intends to do God's own will right here on earth as it is in heaven, then it is *hope*, not fear, that changes what church is for, what church is about, and what church is meant to *do.*

As theologian Jurgen Moltmann wrote, "Those who hope in Christ can no longer put up with reality as it is, but begin to suffer under it, to contradict it. Peace with God means conflict with the world, for the goad of the promised future stabs inexorably into the flesh of every unfulfilled present."[2] Faithful hope begins with a divinely inspired dissatisfaction with the way things are. Faithful hope is a future-oriented existence powered by a present, committed calling to see things made well here and now, and a historically grounded trust that who God has been for our ancestors, God will be for us.

The biblical witness shows us faithful hope at work. The prophet Isaiah, for example, speaks to a people leveled by the power of a neighboring imperial nation and gutted by the subsequent domination under which they were forced to live. Recall that God's people had lost everything they'd built, including their temple, the center of their identity and unity and their physical symbol of God's presence. Their leaders were murdered, their communities exiled to a strange land, and their hope destroyed. The prophet Isaiah, boldly and with what must have been tremendous courage, speaks words that surely seemed ludicrous to anyone within earshot:

---

[2] Jürgen Moltmann, *Theology of Hope: On the Ground and the Implications of a Christian Eschatology* (Minneapolis: Fortress Press, 1993), 21.

> Comfort, comfort my people! says your God. Speak compassionately to Jerusalem, and proclaim to her that her compulsory service has ended, that her penalty has been paid, that she has received from the LORD's hand double for all her sins! A voice is crying out: "Clear the LORD's way in the desert! Make a level highway in the wilderness for our God! Every valley will be raised up, and every mountain and hill will be flattened. Uneven ground will become level, and rough terrain a valley plain. The LORD's glory will appear, and all humanity will see it together; LORD's mouth has commanded it." (Isaiah 40:1–5)

Isaiah goes on to communicate a message from God: "Look, I'm doing a new thing! Now it sprouts up. Don't you recognize it?" (Isaiah 43:19). I'm doing something new *now*, not later, or someday and somewhere else, or with other people, but here, now, where *you* can see it and be part of making it happen.

"I'm making a way in the desert, paths in the wilderness," Isaiah proclaims, as if the utterly unbelievable is already on its way. These are the words of a holy disruptor unwilling to accept a future without hope. These are the words that should animate and stir our own faith practices.

God's people knew that when Isaiah made these declarations, the prophet was referencing the Exodus, where God made a way for the people through the wilderness. The Holy One provided both miraculous rescue and sustenance in a situation cruelly despairing and beyond their ability to summon hope. *Don't you remember?* the prophet asks. *God has done it before and God will do it again!*

Remembering these words, promises of hope in situations where hope doesn't even appear on the list of options, is a beautiful way to cross the bounds of time. They send encouragement to people like us who are searching for the strength to proclaim and follow an unlikely trail toward repair … toward hope. How can we, people also longing for hope, forget the beautiful intersection of the faith of our ancestors and the needs of this present moment?

The answer is that we cannot. We must not. People of faith who have worked so hard to found and maintain institutions now face a critical choice. It's a choice between an eschatology of destruction and an eschatology of hope.

We can, of course, gather whomever we can convince to hang onto the familiar along with us until it's all over, determined to show up in our sanctuaries and denominational meetings as we always have. But those voices that would tell us our only chance is to find some way off this sin-filled planet in the end are voices of eschatological despair. And, as the prophet Isaiah so eloquently reminds us, we have another option.

As people of faith, we can put our hands and hearts and resources toward the work of *tikkun olam*, toward repair. In this version of eschatological living, we do not deny the evil and destruction and violence of this world. We choose, instead, to move with courage toward a future of repair, of justice and wholeness for all our neighbors, in keeping with God's intention for creation.

People who prefer to hurtle through space on a planet destined for destruction might find those committed to healing *this* world untenable disruptors. And they may be right, because efforts to upend systems that provide easy answers and comfort for the powerful have been and will always cause painful disruption.

Hopeful disruption, we would counter, because claiming the words of Jesus to bring God's Kingdom to come on earth as it is in heaven is the very definition of hopeful disruption.

***

Imagine: St. Liborious Catholic Church was a soaring cathedral on the west side of St. Louis. Established by German immigrants in 1856, its red brick, gothic architecture dominated the landscape of East St. Louis upon its completion in 1889. The parish flourished so much that it built a convent, a school, and a rectory. Its imposing edifice dominated the St. Louis landscape for many years. In 1970 it was listed on the National Register of Historic Places, and in 1975 the church's buildings were declared a city landmark.

As white flight took the neighborhood population north, the congregation dwindled and tried everything it could to keep the church alive. Multiple mergers were undertaken, and the church and school buildings were used for income-producing purposes. However, all of these faithful attempts to keep St. Liborious alive just couldn't manage to recreate the grandeur of its past. In 1992 the church was sold, and little by little, the decorative pieces accumulated in that holy space were auctioned off.

A few years later, the sanctuary of that grand cathedral was turned into a skate park called SK8 Liborious. Teenagers who'd previously skated in public parks now flocked to an indoor skate park, complete with ramps to enable flips over what had been the altar, and throughout the edifice, all over the walls, graffiti.[3]

It's true that the abandoned church building then held some purpose, but Sk8 Liborious doesn't exist anymore either. In 2023 a devastating fire caused by faulty wiring in the rectory next door to the cathedral burned that cathedral and its surrounding buildings down to blackened timbers and remaining masonry.

Sk8 Liborious still hopes to rebuild. Meanwhile, the wreckage of that once beautiful church stands as a reminder of the wisdom literature of Ecclesiastes: "There's a season for everything and a time for every matter under the heavens: a time for giving birth and a for dying, a time for planting and a time for uprooting what was planted, a time for killing and a time for healing, a time for tearing down and a time for building up" (Ecclesiastes 3:1–3).

Although this is not the end of this story, it seems right to pause to acknowledge the deep, heavy grief that must have been carried by so many who had a hand in building such a grand edifice and tirelessly supporting the ministries that made up St. Liborious in its heyday.

---

[3] Rachel Chapman, "We Turned an Abandoned Church into a Skatepark. Then Tragedy Struck," *New York Times,* August 17, 2023, https://www.nytimes.com/2023/08/17/opinion/skatepark-community-stlouis-sk8-liborius.html.

And the fear that reading a story like this one will raise in so many of us must be acknowledged: a fear of loss. Loss of our familiar faith expression and community as they always have been, as long as we can remember.

The fear comes from more than the loss of a building because, as we've established, our churches are so much more than the buildings that house them. They are physical places and dear communities where we note the landmarks of our lives … and the grief of their change and, in this case, their loss, can be devastating, raising questions of meaning and belonging. *Who am I without this place?*

Recently, Pastor Amy visited the St. Liborious site. As she stood on the corner of Market and Hogan streets, taking in the site of the burned-out cathedral, a rental car pulled up and parked at the curb just across the street in front of what was formerly the church school, now a juvenile detention center.

An elderly couple climbed out of the car, looking around in disbelief at what must have looked to them like the wreckage of war.

Turning to Pastor Amy, the gentleman explained with tears in his eyes, "I haven't been here in over fifty years. I wanted to show my wife where our family went to church, where I celebrated my first communion, where I went to elementary school."

While the man's wife rummaged through her handbag for a tissue, he said apologetically, "I just feel so sad."

This beautiful and painful exchange was a tangible experience by which to remember that advocating for hopeful disruption in response to the decline of our institutions does not negate the grief of a familiar past gone. The tears continued unabated.

What that elderly couple did not notice at first, however, was the next chapter of this story. In a riotous garden on the lot right next door to the burned-out cathedral, there were diverse people bustling in and out of a gate to which was attached a hand-lettered sign that reads, "New Roots Urban Farm."

***

Imagine: Directly across the street from the juvenile detention center and immediately next door to the destroyed cathedral, Antajuan Adams and Mina Aria have created an urban farm. "I grew up in this neighborhood," Antajuan explains. "My grandma taught me how to grow vegetables. I decided that every kid in this neighborhood should have a safe place to come and learn how to grow their own food."

Antajuan and Mina's original idea has blossomed, even and maybe most especially in the shadow of the skeletal cathedral next door. On any given day, New Roots Urban Farm is filled with volunteer construction crews building elevated beds to provide uncontaminated soil in the wake of the fire, church groups setting up tables out front with sandwiches and cold drinks, an artist or two helping kids and passersby learn to screenprint their own T-shirts that read "Black Farmers Matter," and neighbors from down the block and retirees from other neighborhoods working side by side to weed vegetable patches, making room for the growing cadre of bunnies, geese, chickens, and ducks, even occasionally a goat or two.

Several times a month, big buses with bright-eyed college students pull up to hear Antajuan's story and to see with their own eyes that repair can happen … that repair is happening right now, in the very place that once only held destruction.

Producing and providing safe and nutritious food in a neighborhood where this kind of food is often unattainable is critically important to Antajuan and Mina, who see their work as combating an unjust, apartheid-like system of food production and availability in our country. A former abandoned lot, New Roots Urban Farm leases their land from the city for $1 per year; they've just signed another lease on an abandoned property just around the corner. Right there, still in the shadow of the crumbling St. Liborious cathedral, the farm's expansion of New Roots Urban Orchard is already coming to life.

In addition to all of this work, Antajuan is insistent that in and among the beds of veggies, all kinds of wildflowers grow, filling the space with boisterous color. He will not allow visitors to New Roots Urban Farm to leave without their arms filled with a beautiful bouquet cut from the garden.

Grief is real. But how can we possibly forget that the central story of our faith is death—and resurrection? What might happen if we wiped our tears and grabbed a wheelbarrow to jump in and lend a hand? What would happen is that we could, perhaps to our great surprise, become … the Church anew.[4]

In 1 Corinthians 15 the apostle Paul tries to articulate what life after death will be like:

> But someone will say, "How are the dead raised? What kind of body will they have when they come back?" Look, fool! When you put a seed into the ground, it doesn't come back to life unless it dies. What you put in the ground doesn't have the shape that it will have, but it's a bare grain of wheat or some other seed. God gives it the sort of shape that he chooses, and he gives each of the seeds its own shape. (1 Corinthians 15:35–38)

Look, foolish ones clinging to what has been! Death is necessary, and new life doesn't look like the life that came before it. Maybe new life looks like an urban farm bursting with community connections and abundant crops next to a burnt-out cathedral. Who knows what the Divine has in mind? The form that new life takes is not really up to us; it's up to God.

All we know for sure, in faith, is that new life *will* come. Such hope, theologian Jurgen Moltmann proclaimed, "*makes the Church the source of continual new impulses* towards the realization of righteousness, freedom, and humanity here in the light of the promised future that is to come" (emphasis added).[5]

If we church folk have the fortitude to be honest, we know there is nothing actually sharp or even sudden about the turn religious institutions have taken. As we've established, polls have tracked decline

---

[4] Listen to what Antajuan has to say about that: Invested Faith Fund (@investedfaith), "Meet Invested Faith Fellow Antajuan Adams of New Roots Urban Farm in St. Louis, Missouri," Instagram, October 4, 2024, https://www.instagram.com/reel/DAtC8MWOv73/?igsh=dWt2dm50Njlvb3lw.

[5] Jürgen Moltmann, *Theology of Hope*, 22.

in church membership, religious identity, and many other trends signaling to us for years that the church we find so familiar is quickly becoming a thing of the past.[6] And, in true institutional fashion, we have largely applied our efforts to reinforcing the status quo instead of keeping "our hearts and our churches inured to the sin of scarcity and focused instead on the vast abundance of God".[7] Many of us have taken this route of maintenance over adventure.

But not all of us.

***

In 2022, Rev. Patrick Chandler was tasked by the church he serves, St. Peter's United Church of Christ in Ferguson, Missouri, to help its leadership consider how they might faithfully steward the substantial assets in the church's possession. The church owns of one of the largest cemeteries in greater St. Louis; regular income from that resource helps to fund church programming, along with the income earned from the interest of a substantial endowment.

Located in an area of St. Louis drained by white flight and further injured by the events surrounding the 2014 murder of Michael Brown, the worshiping community has watched decline happen all around them, and the numbers in their pews have not been immune. The church, once a center of lively German immigrant life, over the years became smaller and less able to continue the programming that defined their heyday.

Always a faith community attuned toward the future, even prior to the events their community suffered in 2014, the church leadership decided to build a resource center adjacent to the church. Under the direction of a parish nurse, programs to support the health of the community flourish, including a free mental health clinic, support

---

[6] "In U.S., Decline of Christianity Continues at Rapid Pace," Pew Research, October 17, 2019, https://www.pewresearch.org/religion/2019/10/17/in-u-s-decline-of-christianity-continues-at-rapid-pace/.

[7] Amy Butler, "Investing Faithfully: Planting Seeds of Change," *The Presbyterian Outlook*, September 20, 2022, http://pres-outlook.org/2022/09/investing-faithfully-planting-seeds-of-change/.

for new mothers, and a fathers' grief support group led by Michael Brown Sr.

These and other impactful community programs thrive at St. Peter's, enthusiastically encouraged by the now smaller congregation and supported by the significant funds they were tasked with directing. Still, Pastor Patrick Chandler knew his congregation likely would never return to the bustling community of yesteryear. Accepting and helping his community embrace their new identity, as a scrappy group of holy disruptors, has become his task as leader.

After learning about the work of Invested Faith and sharing conversation about new possibilities for seeding the future of the church, Rev. Chandler agreed to a visit from Pastor Amy. She arrived in Ferguson and spent the day touring the church, dropping in at the resource center, and visiting the gravesite of Michael Brown Jr. in the cemetery owned by St. Peter's.

Over a meal discussing next steps, Rev. Chandler, in his direct and no-nonsense way, asked Pastor Amy, "What do you want?"

She replied, "A million dollars."

To Rev. Chandler's eternal credit, he didn't even flinch when asked for a gift of that substantial size. Together, Pastor Amy and Rev. Chandler began a two-year process of introducing St. Peter's to the work of Invested Faith, building relationships between the congregation and Invested Faith Fellows in the larger St. Louis area, and collaboratively painting a picture of a future fueled by the gifts of the past.

In 2024 the congregation of St. Peter's United Church of Christ voted to give that gift of one million dollars, courageously setting an example for other churches.[8] This money, given by St. Peter's to the Invested Faith Fund, serves as the anchor gift to start a fund for

---

[8] Learn more about the St. Peter's gift here: "Invested Faith and St. Peter's United Church of Christ Announce Million Dollar Gift," Invested Faith, September 10, 2024, https://www.investedfaith.org/news/invested-faith-st-peters-ucc-million-dollar-gift.

churches with similar resources ready to invest in the future and for congregations completing their ministry and looking for a meaningful legacy tool to send their witness forward.

Another beautiful example of a faith community willing to take a risk to seed the future is animated by the story of Bethel United Church of Christ in Arlington, Virginia. For over eighty years the church with the red doors on Arlington Boulevard marked a place of welcome to the neighborhood. Bethel United Church of Christ was founded in 1941 as the suburb of Arlington was growing. As the church prepared to break ground and build, the United States entered World War II and the building was postponed. The community, however, was not; Bethel worshiped together as a community devoted to welcoming their neighbors.

And Bethel saw neighbors everywhere—next door and across the globe. Each generation brought its own service to the congregation, beginning with famous turkey dinners for those soldiers stationed at Arlington Hall during World War II, an effort that both helped raise money to build the sanctuary after the war and provided a community for those serving. The congregation invested in the Arlington community through local organizations like the Arlington Food Assistance Center, beginning with bagging groceries then supporting the center financially. Through relationships over the years, Bethel was instrumental in the creation of both a school in Uganda and a medical clinic in a small town in El Salvador.

As Arlington grew, the church faced issues of adapting the property to the modern era, with challenges like finding enough parking on Sunday mornings, and in 2018 the congregation left their building and moved in with Arlington Church of the Brethren nearby. Along with time came the same challenges that many congregations are now facing: fewer people joining worship on Sunday mornings, fewer still available to help manage the life of an active congregation, and the difficulty of finding and employing a pastor to lead in bold and innovative ways.

Finally, the congregation made the difficult and courageous decision to complete their worshiping life together. But it was obvious that Bethel would live on in the decisions they'd made over the years about how they steward their assets. The saints of the past and neighbors of the future would be woven together through the Bethel legacy committee's distributions of financial assets.

In choosing how to distribute the assets, the legacy committee kept Bethel's expansive understanding of "neighbor" in mind. Gifts were given to those partnerships the church had maintained through its history, as well as to association and denominational bodies that had supported the church over time. With the sale of the church property, the legacy committee was able to make a gift of seventy-five thousand dollars to Invested Faith. This gift means the Bethel legacy lives on through the far-reaching work of Invested Faith Fellows all over the United States.[9]

One part of this faith community's life together has ended, yet Bethel is still here. They are empowering the church's evolving witness in the world, moving us toward the beautiful dream that Jesus kept trying to tell us about: the Kingdom of God. Bethel is here in each and every Invested Faith Fellow who, thanks to Bethel's legacy gift, is able to build a business that brings new life to a community.

***

This is church.

We know that church is changing. Still, we need examples of traditional churches like St. Peter's and Bethel, ready to step out and take the risk of a future we cannot yet see but believe with all our hearts that God is creating. The work of God in the world was happening long before our buildings were built in the years when churches were booming. And the work of God in the world will certainly continue long after we're gone. Congregations able to embrace an emerging reality are leading the way.

---

[9] For traditional churches unable to shift in this moment, Invested Faith offers an impactful legacy tool powered by the assets of faith communities at the end of their institutional lives, congregations at completion. By donating some of their assets to help Invested Faith build this fund, traditional churches are building a legacy that will live long past them.

We can't stop thinking about Jesus and his invitation to just throw out those seeds of goodness and justice in the world. His "sower of the seeds" parable is an embodiment of Christian hope.[10] The way Jesus tells it, the optimistic farmer scatters seed everywhere, as if it costs nothing. Some seeds falls on the path, which was unprepared to receive it; some fall among the rocks, which seems good at first but isn't; some even fall amidst the thorny weeds, which don't give an inch to the seeds, no way, no how. But some fall in rich, beautiful soil, and the harvest from that is more than enough to make up for the seeds lost to less ideal places. When the yield comes, it is miraculous abundance no one could have predicted.

Imagine this parable read aloud in the community of the early church. Remember they heard this story of Jesus while they navigated Roman rule, religious oppression, and the destruction of the temple, as well as economic hardship. Our spiritual ancestors listened while they wrestled with questions about who would be in and who would be out in their communities, and while they struggled to understand how they were to go forward with this new faith without their leader's physical presence. In the midst of their context, we wonder what it was like for them to hear this parable of experimentation, risk, imagination, and miraculous reward. Did it sound as preposterous to them to just start flinging seeds around as it sometimes sounds to us?

Yet the story's truths are the same. It's not our job to worry too much about where those seeds land and whether or how they grow. It's our job, instead, to keep our hearts and our churches inured to the sin of scarcity and focused instead on the vast abundance of God. What an incredible gift to notice and celebrate that in this moment we are stewards of much of that abundance, to be used to plant seeds for the future of faith communities and the healing of the world. How very, very hopeful.

---

[10] See Mark 4:1–9, Matthew 13:1–9, Luke 8:4–8.

Though your destination is not yet clear
You can trust the promise of this opening;
Unfurl yourself into the grace of beginning
That is at one with your life's desire.
Awaken your spirit to adventure;
Hold nothing back, learn to find ease in risk;
Soon you will be home in a new rhythm,
For your soul senses the world that awaits you.

—John O'Donohue[1]

[1] John O'Donohue, "For a New Beginning," in *To Bless the Space Between Us: A Book of Blessings* (United States: Doubleday, 2008), 14. Reprinted with permission from Penguin Random House.

CHAPTER 10

Becoming Holy Disruptors

The stories you've read here will not be the same stories your faith community will live. You have your own context, distinct in myriad ways from those we've described in this book. The synergy of believing in God's ongoing work, embracing a theology of hope and abundance, and taking steps you never imagined make up the content of your unique story. And therein lies perhaps the hardest part of living into a future we cannot see. Tempting as it is to find an idea that might work and adopt it as your own, the process of dreaming a future together with the Holy Spirit is where the difficult spiritual work comes to the fore.

Who knows what holy disruption is ahead for you? You could be like a church in Oakland, California, using their fellowship hall to create housing for citizens returning from incarceration. Maybe you're like a congregation near a river in Ohio starting a "citizen scientists" program to test that water weekly and advocate for change. Or perhaps your community is more suited to be like a church in Austin, Texas, that is selling their historic building to build a high-rise multi-use building with their church on the first floor.

Perhaps. But don't forget that there is no effective plan called "Five Steps to Returning Your Church to 1954." We've told you these stories as a starting place for your imagination to take root, for you to join the holy disruptors determined to use what they have to heal and repair a world in deep need. It's *your* imagination God wants to see, and more than that, it's the courage it takes to live into that imagination that will birth within you the urgency of holy disruption, the seeds of change.

If your community finds the gumption to think outside the box and take on the role of holy disruptors, we cannot tell you exactly how that will happen. What we can suggest are some intentional actions—spiritual practices, you might call them—that taken seriously will disrupt, discomfort, and completely transform what seemed before to be a hopeless cause.

Jesus did not do the work of repairing the world alone, and neither can we. It will take all of us together to cultivate seeds of imagination so that our faith communities might burst beyond the confines of what has been and emerge transformed.

People of faith, we have allowed ourselves to be distracted and fractured by the urgency and pain of trying too hard to recreate a familiar past. But now is a moment of immense opportunity. If we will marry the faithfulness of our God who will never leave us with all the courage we can summon, we can become holy disruptors ourselves. We can lead the way for those who come behind us, showing the world that the work of God is alive and well. We can repair—stitch by stitch—the fragments of a world in tatters. We can make holy disruption our spiritual practice, for such a time as this.[1]

Here are some ways to begin:

Cultivate an urgent dissatisfaction with the status quo.

Tiffany Terrell with Better Way Grocers repeatedly noticed the health effects of a lack of fresh food for the families in her daycare business. It bothered her. A lot. When she scratched the surface to see why the people she cared about were suffering from asthma, diabetes, and obesity from young ages, she discovered that convenience stores were the only grocery stores within a reasonable distance from the families she served. Tiffany found that reality unacceptable. She addressed the problem head-on by learning about the crisis she observed, by attending a conference on food injustice in our country, and by cultivating a stubborn refusal to accept things the way they were. If you ask her now, she'll tell you that she never expected to

[1] See Esther 4:14.

own a mobile grocery store making ten stops a week throughout the neighborhoods where her families live so they could have access to affordable, convenient, fresh food.

Josh Richardson through Brugmansia Ministries can't bring himself to pay less than full attention to the groans of the planet. And he is also listening hard to the echoing silence of people of faith, the lack of attention and urgency faith communities spend preparing for the coming impact of climate change. Who is preparing faith communities for mass migration? How are we ensuring that safe water is a resource available to our neighbors? Why does solar energy never appear on the Trustee Board's agenda? This stunning lack of attention to the realities of climate change and the impact that change will have on faith communities would not let him rest; the pressing dissatisfaction he felt with the situation bothered him so much that he ditched his paid profession to lead a ministry of resilience planning for churches. Urgency compelled him to do everything he can to right the ship before it's too late. He could not just shrug and say "oh well."

Moy Mendez is a caring pastor who listens to his people. When he found himself praying after worship with person after person who asked for prayer because they couldn't pay their rent, an urgent dissatisfaction planted itself in his heart. Praying with people stuck in a disempowering economic system of poverty is a powerful tool. But a community of faith taking action, acting as the hands and feet of the Divine, soon became more than a "what if." When praying a prayer and leaving things exactly as they are will not suffice, that urgent dissatisfaction becomes the work of God in the world. In Moy's case, this was the moment that The Hope Center became an answer to prayer.

New life starts with an acknowledgement that in the world God dreams for us, what is, is not what should be. It moves to paying attention to who in your immediate vicinity is suffering and why, then curates that urgent dissatisfaction until it pushes us to look harder at how we can be agents of change. God's kingdom come, God's will be done, on earth as it is in heaven, remember? Let that urgent dissatisfaction burrow deep into your heart so that ignoring the ills you have the power to change will not let you rest until you take action to make meaningful change for your community.

Notice your abundant resources.

In a culture of decline for our institutions, we are automatically preconditioned to see what we have through a lens of scarcity. We don't have enough volunteers. … We don't have the ministries we had twenty years ago. … We don't have enough young families/children/teenagers, etc. While scarcity may be the lens through which many religious institutions are looking at this moment, that view is factually incorrect. In fact, nearly ten years ago, in 2016, *The Guardian* published an article positing that religious institutions in the United States possess more assets than Apple, Amazon, and Google combined.[2] Your institution's facilities, your finances, your strengths, your people, your cache in your communities, your years of witness and care for countless families—all of these are all tremendous resources at your disposal. Untold hours and numerous talents have been placed in our care for the purpose of living in the way of Jesus. Take a look around and make a list of everything your faith community possesses. Just try it. When you do, you will be astonished at the plenty available for your very own holy disruption.

Village Green RVA was born because a congregation looked at their vacuous church building and thought, *Can't we be better stewards of all this space?* That previously empty space has become the headquarters of a huge community collaboration that serves their neighbors in need.

And when Jessica David realized the tremendous investment capital of the community foundation where she worked might be invested for social change rather than bolstering corporations on Wall Street, a seed was planted that keeps on growing. Local Return and the Rhode Island Investment Corporation are now using financial resources for true good in local communities.

---

[2] Harriet Sherwood, "Religion in US 'Worth More Than Google and Apple Combined,'" *The Guardian*, September 15, 2016, https://www.theguardian.com/world/2016/sep/15/us-religion-worth-1-trillion-study-economy-apple-google.

Chelsea Spyres and the four churches of the Wilmington Kitchen Collective realized that church commercial kitchens going unused 99 percent of the time were untapped resources. They offered those kitchens to the community, flinging them out as seeds into the soil of God's economy. With all available resources now in use, we wonder when other churches will recognize their resources and make space for the forty-plus food truck entrepreneurs now on the WKC waiting list!

Notice what God has given you and how you are stewarding it. As Jesus asked the disciples when they were faced with the challenge of four thousand mouths to feed, "How much bread do you have?" (Matthew 15:34). Churches rarely close because they run out of money! They close because they run out of people and energy for ministry. Pray about how to connect your abundant resources to innovative ministry.

Don't just strategize about how your institution will survive; plan for how it will die so that others may live!

Our job is not to preserve the present; it's to plant seeds for the future. According to the research of church consultant Carey Nieuwhouf, church closures in 2023 appeared to be outpacing new church plants 3–1, with roughly ten thousand churches closing each year in the United States and three thousand new churches being planted. Nieuwhof says, "That's an untenable ratio if we want the future of the church to be vibrant".[3] If you're thinking of launching a new ministry, the need is great.

When Connection Christian Church was First Christian Church, I, Pastor Dawn, was praying with my husband and colleague, Pastor Joe, to lead the congregation to something new. The primary temptation for the church's leadership was to focus primarily on caring for people already in the congregation. Making sure people we already loved were well taken care of was a time-consuming and

---

[3] Carey Nieuwhof, "Disruptive Church Trends That Will Rule 2025," Carey Nieuwhof, December 5, 2024, https://careynieuwhof.com/wp-content/uploads/2024/12/5-Disruptive-Church-Trends-That-Will-Rule-2025-Leader-Guide.pdf.

strong centripetal force, pulling the church inadvertently toward self-centeredness.

One of our first steps to redevelop hearts turned outward, toward our neighbors, was the practice of Ashes to Go. Ashes to Go has become common all over the world.[4] It is a simple Ash Wednesday offering of ashes and prayer to passersby in unusual locations. We adopted this practice because we needed not only to serve our neighbors again, but also to *see* our neighbors again. We needed to notice who God had placed in our paths as neighbors we are called to love. So we set up shop on Ash Wednesday outside a grocery store, a gas station, a fast food restaurant, in a hospital chapel, and on a busy street corner. A small group of church leaders took turns joining in the effort.

We were amazed at the receptivity to our invitation to receive a blessing with ashes and prayer. Some made an indelible impression, like the man who saw us as he was grocery shopping and went back to load up his aged mother in the car so she could also be blessed, and the woman who was on her way to take a child with special needs to the doctor who pulled over to ask for prayer. After serving for an hour or so at each location, we concluded our time there by naming each person we had encountered and lifting them up in prayer. Our hearts were broken open by meeting our neighbors.

Soon we started a weekly Bible study at Homemade Wines, a neighborhood wine bar. We offered small group gatherings at Chick-fil-A and at a grocery store. We met monthly around tables at Zucchi's restaurant as a "dinner church" model. We held communion at a park, where we offered a potluck to the whole neighborhood. We had evening gatherings at a local coffee shop with storytelling and book clubs. We created a tutoring and snacks ministry for children that gathered in the community room of a local apartment complex on a weeknight. We started a monthly gathering in our county's juvenile detention center for the youth and staff there.

When the congregation began to fall in love again the possibilities of the impact we could make in our community, when we began to

---

[4] You can learn more about"Ashes to Go" at https://ashestogo.org/

see the way we could change the lives of our neighbors, the centrifugal force of reaching out to others finally pulled us out of ourselves. *We began to make decisions not just to preserve our existence as a congregation but decisions that would be life-giving to those far beyond the church's core members.* By the time we moved into our church's new location and opened our nonprofits center, you could see by the activities on our church calendar that this congregation loved the neighbors who weren't yet a part of our church as much as we loved the people in our church. God had changed our hearts to look outward as well as inward, to die to ourselves so that others could live.

Once people of faith remember that people outside the walls of our faith communities are the *very people we exist to serve*, being a thriving, creative faith community becomes more possible. It turns out God's commissioning of Abram still holds: we are indeed blessed in order to be a blessing.[5]

Dream together.

When we allow injustice to pester us enough to break our hearts, when we assess the resources we already have in our hands, when we are willing to let things die so that others may live, then we are ready to imagine what perhaps could be.

As we've said, Jesus encouraged faithful imagination with his stories. Remember the story of the mustard seed? It's the smallest of seeds, but it grows into such a large tree that birds enjoy building their nests in it.[6] It's nearly impossible to see a large tree hosting birds from just looking at a tiny mustard seed. But a divinely inspired imagination can take us there. Walter Bruggemann writes about holy disruptors, or prophets:

> The prophet engages in futuring fantasy. The prophet does not ask if the vision can be implemented, for questions of implementation are of no consequence until the vision can be imagined. The imagination must come before the implementation. Our culture is competent to implement

[5] See Genesis 12:3.

[6] See Mark 4:30–32; Matthew 13:31–32.

> almost anything and to imagine almost nothing. The same royal consciousness that makes it possible to implement anything and everything is the one that shrinks imagination because imagination is a danger. Thus every totalitarian regime is frightened of the artist. It is the vocation of the prophet to keep alive the ministry of imagination, to keep on conjuring and proposing futures alternative to the single one the king wants to urge as the only thinkable one.[7]

Before we can implement plans, we must imagine what is possible. Imagination is the work of prayer and walks around the neighborhood. It's the stuff of art projects and music, of looking out the window at the birds in the trees. It's reading poetry and watching children play together. Imagination can't be rushed. Imagination has to be nurtured, given permission, and coaxed into being.

So many of Jesus' stories are told to help us develop and exercise our imaginations. How else were his friends supposed to hang on through everything that met their physical eyes with such harsh realities of poverty and oppression, crucifixions and crackdowns? They needed to see with their mind's eye, to behold in their hearts the possibilities that were inside of a mustard seed. Throughout this book, we've invited you to imagine. Keep imagining with our holy disruptors …

Leslee Matthews can imagine a world where women and girls no longer need to be afraid. She can see the day when gender-based violence is no more. Leslee began imagining this when she was ten years old, and the vision compels her even decades later. It's a vision that she and SOUL Law Firm have taken to the state supreme court.

Jon Adam Ross can imagine a world where people with diametrically opposed worldviews are coaxed into exploring each other's perspectives while they create together. He can see them building relationships across divides because they have taken the time to understand one another. It's a vision that Inheritance Theater Project has taken around the country in multiple venues in diverse communities.

---

[7] Walter Brueggemann,. *The Prophetic Imagination:40th Anniversary Edition* (Minneapolis: Fortress Press, 2018), 40.

Pastor Cue and The Row faith community have such a vivid imagination that they put the Hip Hop Smoothie Shop on Skid Row! They are insistent that people living in this impoverished area can be treated well in their employment and have dignity in their nutrition. They imagine a flourishing garden of personal agency and self-esteem growing in the concrete jungle.

When Rev. Dustin Mailman experienced the loss of his friend Phoenix to a drug overdose, he knew that her inability to get employment because of her status as a felon led to her tragic death. He channeled his grief to imagine what he could build that Phoenix once needed. Deep Time was born to give other returning citizens the chance Phoenix didn't have.

It is our prayer that the stories in this book have jump-started your imagination. Take time—not just thirty minutes in a meeting, but a *season* for prayerful imagination. Ask God for eyes to see what he wants you to see—what is there and what is not there that could be. In the words of Walter Brueggemann, "Our faith comes to fullness as we are teased to think new thoughts, as our imagination is lured beyond 'business as usual.'"[8]

Begin now, not later.

Beverly Jenkins saw an abandoned mall, prayed about it, and scribbled a drawing of the five community resources that a transformation of that huge, abandoned space might house. That mall is now the Refuge and Restoration Marketplace. Beverly tells people who ask her how they did it that it began with just one step. Just start, she says. There are plenty of excuses for not trying. Don't wait for a better time, a different price, or a more ideal situation. Just begin taking steps toward the risk you are willing to take in order to move into new life. To remind her, Beverly plans to have that scratch paper framed and hung on the wall!

That's what Jen Owens did after she hosted two refugee families for Thanksgiving dinner. She got to know more refugee women in

---

[8] Walter Brueggemann, *Living Toward a Vision: Biblical Reflections on Shalom* (Cleveland: Pilgrim Press, 1982), 11.

her community and developed connections with them. Soon she was making jewelry and sewing items alongside the women, offering their products at pop-up sales at friends' houses. The substantial business of Forai took off from those humble beginnings.

Josh Richardson didn't have time to waste. His health crisis made it clear that he needed to make the difference he intended to make with his life with whatever time he still has. The urgency of responding proactively to climate change called to him. Josh quit his job and jumped into offering his scientific skills and theological training to churches who were ready to get it: Climate change is happening, and the best time to start preparing for it was yesterday. Ministry as resilience became Josh's rallying cry.

Robert Rueda wanted to help students at his university, but he had no idea how to begin or how long they could keep a pay-what-you-can restaurant going. Someone offered to donate enough money to buy two months' worth of purchase orders. He thought to himself, *Well, let's give it a go for two months, and if it ends, at least we did it for two months*. Now they have been going for seven years, serving about 1,200 students a month! All because they just started somewhere, took the first step, and kept going.

Professor Kenda Creasy Dean urges us,

> Missional innovation will not save the church. Only Jesus Christ saves the church. But you could make the case that Jesus' first followers were an entrepreneurial lot, gathering familiar religious teachings in unimagined ways that gave rise to entirely new faith communities, patterned on the self-giving love they saw embodied in the life, death, and resurrection of Jesus Christ—and that should give us abundant permission to do the same. Finally, we may lament the current condition of the institutional church—yet I consider this to be the church's best opportunity in 500 years to be reshaped into the church we are called to be.[9]

---

[9] Kenda Creasy Dean, "Why Churches Should Be Talking More About Social Entrepreneurship," *Caring Magazine*, August 31, 2017, https://caringmagazine.org/churches-talking-social-entrepreneurship/.

In other words, you may have to wait another five hundred years for a better time to begin than now. Start somewhere new doing something good as soon as possible. The Holy Spirit will help you find your footing. Just take a step.

Ask only a few for permission, but ask everyone for partnerships.

Sometimes our momentum is delayed because we care a lot about what everyone thinks about what we are doing. Depending on the polity of your faith community, it can be grueling to gain consensus for change. But you are not looking for 100 percent agreement, are you? That's not possible in an organization filled with human beings. Get permission where you must, but don't let the tyranny of the minority clog up your process.[10]

You don't need to ask everyone for permission, but you do need to ask everyone you can think of for partnership. Partnerships bring expertise, resources, ideas, and synergy that you won't otherwise have on your own. As the Christian Community Development Association remarks on its website:

> Effective community development often requires the cooperation of the public, private, and social sectors. We have far too long gone it alone, and we need each other! Faith communities engaging in social entrepreneurship **can** serve as bridges, bringing together diverse stakeholders for the common good. The impact of cross-sector collaboration in this process cannot be overstated.[11]

Emanuel "Boo" Milton could see that his community was fractured in ways that were hurting everyone. Rampant drug problems and conflict with law enforcement in the community called for some

---

[10] More on this in Pastor Dawn's book *Breakthrough: Trusting God with Big Change in Your Church* (St. Louis: Chalice Press, 2002), in chapter 4, as explained by Rev. Dr. Joe Weaks.

[11] Andre Towner, "Redefining the Role of Faith Communities Through Social Entrepreneurship," Christian Community Development Center, April 9, 2024, https://ccda.org/redefining-the-role-of-faith-communities-through-social-entrepreneurship/.

way to bring everyone together to heal the problems they faced. Boo decided that Cure With Love Strategies, his social enterprise, would host a city-wide dodgeball tournament. Boo openly invited the people who help shape the city from all walks of life, but Boo would assign the teams. With intentional wisdom, employees of the police department and suspected drug dealers were assigned to spend a day working together as teammates. More than a thousand people packed a local gym. A community learned in a very practical and tangible way that when we work together, we're better.

The dodgeball tournament turned into other opportunities for the community to gather, like a Sunday afternoon tea called "Look at God," where the community is invited to show up and share moments of goodness and hope they experienced that week. A group of young adults curious about writing poetry also began meeting together every Monday night to support one another. The power of a community coming together to heal rifts by helping diverse people partner together is the work of God in the world.

It is, in fact, what Jesus did—without the dodgeball, as far as we know.

More examples of partnerships abound: Dr. Kit Evans-Ford works with multiple partners to support the women she serves and to sell the products they make. Argrow's House is part of the Global Share Trade Council for Thistle Farms and a network of about thirty-six sister organizations around the world. Beverly and Ken Jenkins through R & R Marketplace prayerfully connected investors and people-helping organizations from all over the community in order to pull off the miraculous purchase of a mall for ministry. Marisa Prince and Calvin Lee, with the Spirit's help, pulled together a diverse group of people and organizations with talents they need to implement campaigns that vividly express the message of oneness in Christ on multimedia platforms. Dustin Mailman had multiple teachers to lead him in discovering the fine art of roasting coffee beans for Deep Time.

You need partners to teach you what you don't know, to expand your vision beyond what you could think of alone, and to provide skills and resources you don't yet have. Partnering is essential for maximum effectiveness and minimum loneliness on the journey of holy disruption.

Aim for sustainability.

Creative thinkers can and are finding ways to do good and do well at the same time. Doing what makes financial sense and provides economic dignity for everyone involved will sustain ministry. Finding innovative ways to fund good work will build a legacy of thriving that will last long beyond the original seed of an idea.

Drew Nagy knew when he became pastor of Westover Baptist that they could no longer maintain their property and their building with the dwindling participation and disappearing financial support they were facing. But when Living Water Community Center was born, not only did their ministry reach expand, but now their building maintenance costs have decreased and their income stream has diversified. That's good business *and* good church.

Dustin Mailman, while developing Deep Time, created a model for sustainability for that ministry. He discovered that workforce development grants are easily connected to community organizations offering job training to at-risk populations like citizens returning from incarceration. Twenty-five percent of Deep Time's budget is from workforce development reimbursements, which can provide up to 75 percent of the salary for employees in training programs. The rest of Deep Time's budget comes from, in order, selling coffee, customer donations, grants, and the support of Trinity Church.

Robert Rueda is now seven years into building Global Blends into a blessing for others. At this point in their story, Global Blends is not only able to sustain what they are doing in the restaurant, but also able to invest additional income into their larger ministry to students on campus. Global Blends is not just a ministry; it also funds ministry! Diversifying their ministry income stream has meant that their work will last for years to come even if other sources of income wane.

Before Connection Christian Church relocated and opened its nonprofit Connection Center, the congregation was drawing seventy-five thousand dollars a year from its endowment to meet expenses, a common practice but one that was not sustainable indefinitely. But now, because of the growth of the congregation and rental income from their partners, they are able to fund life-changing ministry for decades to come.

New Roots Urban Farm has just signed a lease for 1.75 more acres of land to grow a fruit and nut orchard for their community. The land is nearby, their volunteer base of over three thousand people annually is abundant, and their funding is secure, thanks in part to Invested Faith. They have worked for years to be ready for this expansion, and they are. Now, because of their careful, strategic planning, even more bounty will grow and people will flourish.

Sometimes in ministry we say "God will provide." That spiritual truth is best lived out in wise planning and savvy business models. As you dream, remember that making income to reinvest in your faith community or your ministry is a part of being a good steward.

Trust in resurrection.

Our faith has given us both the challenge and the promises we need to use our lives to bring the story of our shared community to a redemptive conclusion. It's what some of us call salvation.

It's what God did in the story of Jesus when the tomb was empty and the presence of Christ soared beyond the bounds of time and place. It's what Jesus' faith community did when Jesus ascended. They gathered strength from the Holy Spirit's outpouring and started their own ministries of justice and mercy in the name of the risen Christ who could then only be seen through them.

But here's the thing: as articulators of the sacred narrative, we are somewhere in the middle of the story as it is currently being told. And no matter what clergy or other ecclesiological experts may say, we don't know exactly how our part of the story will end. But we are tasked in this moment to push one another to act in faithful ways, to take the risks that faith and radical love require of us, and to live out a theology of hope in tangible, creative ways.

We are at a moment like the one when the Lord takes the prophet Elijah to a valley of dry bones after Israel's defeat and exile. Remember that story?

> The LORD's power overcame me, and while I was in the LORD's spirit, he led me out and set me down in the middle of a certain valley. It was full of bones. He led me through them all around, and I saw that there were a great many of them on the valley floor, and they were very dry.
>
> He asked me, "Human one, can these bones live again?"
>
> I said, "LORD God, only you know."
>
> He said to me, "Prophesy over these bones, and say to them, Dry bones, hear the LORD's word! The LORD God proclaims to these bones: I am about to put breath in you, and you will live again. I will put sinews on you, place flesh on you, and cover you with skin. When I put breath in you, and you come to life, you will know that I am the LORD." (Ezekiel 37:1–6)

Only God knows what comes next in our story. But our work is to trust in resurrection and proclaim, highlight, and resource the hopeful disruption that is on its way.

Fear of failure is real, and facing it will not be easy. But this moment requires us to listen hard to those voices who would remind us of the ever-creating nature of the God we serve. As Walter Brueggeman writes, "Neither the world nor the church needs to stay the way it is, because God is at work who makes all things new."[12]

The church in the United States, along with our larger denominational institutions, is still a powerful force for healing and hope, for the work of the gospel, and for the repair of a world desperate for good news. We cannot and must not ever forget that the work of God continues, very often in ways and in places we don't find familiar. The question for all of us at this moment will define the future of faith institutions in our country: Will we find those places where

---

[12] Walter Brueggemann, *Living Toward a Vision*, 185.

God is at work bringing new life and show up to aid that work with the tremendous resources at our disposal?

No more building bigger barns. No more hoarding resources. No more living as if the present we enjoy is an inviolable holy relic. Like the wealthy man with storehouses of grain, our lives are required of us at this very moment. We pray we are not fools.

We offer this book as a manifesto of hope. We pray it helps us to see the abundant resources that are ours to use to respond to God's invitation to join in the work God is doing in the world. God's work is not dead, or even dying. God is bringing about the restoration of all things and fullness of life often beyond the walls of the Church. God is on the move, disrupting all the safe and comfortable realities we enjoy. Holding on to what used to be will not bring us the joy and meaning available to us when we join God's work in the world. The opportunity for new life is laid out in front of us, just waiting for our response.

Now the story of resurrection is yours to tell and to embody in your unique context. You and your faith community are invited to become holy disruptors, too.

For the hope of the world and the future of gospel-shaped faith communities, we pray your answer is a resounding yes.

Afterword

Seeds … so many thoughts about seeds were swirling in my head and planting themselves in my heart when I, Pastor Amy, sat down in a London coffee shop the next morning to meet a young man whose story I wanted to hear.

This young man was trained to be a pastor, to lead a traditional church through the "11 o'clock Sunday morning, fifth pew on the left, right next to the stained-glass window installed in memory of my grandmother" familiarity we all were trained in. After seminary, he moved back to his family's hometown and took up leadership of a local congregation.

Shortly after he did, tragedy visited his family. His father-in-law, a long-time, blue-collar factory worker in the town, had retired. With no job to go to, no community to surround him, and no meaningful work to fill his days, depression rolled over him like a semi-truck; he died by suicide.

This young minister realized there were men just like his father-in-law all over the town where he lived. They were not finding the community they needed to live full and productive lives outside their lives' work. They were not finding what they needed at church, either.

The story I'm telling you here ends like this. This young minister was so profoundly impacted by the loss his family experienced and the glaring need in his community that he decided to start a business instead of lead a traditional church. He started a brewery, learned to make beer, then taught many in the group of retired men in his community how to brew beer, too.

This story is full of holy moments: retired steel mill workers spending their days in conversation with each other, building a supportive network of friends that sustained them through change, and learning a skill that helped build a business.

How many lonely people did not die by suicide because this young pastor left a pulpit to start a brewery? If the gospel is good news, being shared with all who need to hear it, what if being and building gospel communities can begin with just a little seed like a brewery?

What if people of faith are those who have somehow found the courage to move through the fear, to feel the whisper and wind of the Spirit of God inviting us to imagine, and who do it … who step out believing that God is sometimes like a colorful trail of autumn leaves, painting a path that will lead us somewhere new?

What if?

Small Group Guide

A note from Pastor Amy and Pastor Dawn:

Thank you for taking this journey with us, and especially for choosing not to go it alone. Thank you for gathering with others to read and reflect on the stories in this book.

Because we are pastors and accustomed to walking alongside our people through life changes, we wanted to say that we know this book will likely make you uncomfortable in some places. At least it made us uncomfortable as we wrote it!

We want to walk with you through this process in the most supportive way we can, so we offer this small group guide designed to facilitate powerful and meaningful group reflection and, we hope, courageous action.

In these opportunities for reflection, you will find a welcome exercise and scripture for each session, questions to help you apply the reading, a poem or quote from the book to jump-start your conversations, and a closing prayer experience for each session.

Your faithfulness to even engage these questions inspires us. We see you. We celebrate the time and energy you are giving to see what's next for the future of faith communities in the United States.

Please know that we're praying as hard as we can and imagining as big as we can right alongside you.

With gratitude,

— Pastor Dawn and Pastor Amy

Session 1: Begin Here

(Chapters 1 and 2)

Gather whatever art supplies you have on hand.

Welcome each person and offer thanks for the courage and time of all of the participants. Invite each person to introduce themselves by naming a way that their faith community is important to them.

Read the scripture passage John 12:23–28, taking turns reading a verse aloud at a time:

> Jesus replied, "The time has come for the Human One to be glorified.
>
> I assure you that unless a grain of wheat falls into the earth and dies, it can only be a single seed. But if it dies, it bears much fruit.
>
> Those who love their lives will lose them, and those who hate their lives in this world will keep them forever.
>
> Whoever serves me must follow me. Wherever I am, there my servant will also be. My Father will honor whoever serves me.
>
> "Now *I am deeply troubled.* What should I say? 'Father, save me from this time'? No, for this is the reason I have come to this time.
>
> Father, glorify your name!" Then a voice came from heaven, "I have glorified it, and I will glorify it again."

Ask:

- What are some of the seed stories of Jesus you remember?
- What do you think Jesus was referring to when he said a seed had to fall to the ground and die in order to bear fruit? How have you seen that to be true or untrue?
- Pastor Dawn described a time when church members offered their keys to the church building in the offering plate.

What emotions might they have been experiencing during that moment? What emotions did that story evoke in you?

- What are some of the "unlikely places" where you see signs of new life emerging in faith communities?
- What does it mean to you to be a "holy disruptor"?

Read this quote aloud, followed by a few moments of silence: "Just where we least expect [God], he comes most fully."[1]

Pray by using art supplies to draw, paint, or sculpt a place where God has come where no one expected it. It can be a biblical story, a historical event, or a personal testimony. Invite each person to express briefly where God is in their work of art.

Close by having a leader share this prayer:

"God whose other name seems to be 'surprise,'[2] help us to meet this moment with open eyes and hearts. God who came to us in Jesus Christ, show us how to serve our Savior. God who is with us now in the Holy Spirit, guide our path to find your wisdom always." Amen.

---

[1] Frederick Buechner, "Weekly Sermon Illustration: The Face in the Sky," Frederick Buechner, December 19, 2022, https://www.frederickbuechner.com/weeklysermonillustrations/2022/12/19/weekly-sermon-illustration-the-face-in-the-sky.

[2] John Claypool, "Surprise Is God's Other Name," sermon at Northminster Baptist Church, Jackson, Mississippi, December 3, 1978.

Session 2: Radicalizing Our Resources

(Chapters 3 and 4)

Gather a dry erase board, large newsprint or poster board, and markers.

Welcome each person and give thanks for the contributions each person makes to your faith community. Brainstorm resources the group has. Have each person name two or three personal resources (my house, my car, my education, etc.), continuing through the group, with the goal of as much variety as possible. Write each resource on your board.

Read the scripture passage Matthew 15:29–39, taking turns to read a verse aloud at a time:

> Jesus moved on from there along the shore of the Galilee Sea. He went up a mountain and sat down.
>
> Large crowds came to him, including those who were paralyzed, blind, injured, and unable to speak, and many others. They laid them at his feet, and he healed them.
>
> So the crowd was amazed when they saw those who had been unable to speak talking, and the paralyzed cured, and the injured walking, and the blind seeing. And they praised the God of Israel.
>
> Now Jesus called his disciples and said, "I feel sorry for the crowd because they have been with me for three days and have nothing to eat. I don't want to send them away hungry for fear they won't have enough strength to travel."
>
> His disciples replied, "Where are we going to get enough food in this wilderness to satisfy such a big crowd?"
>
> Jesus said, "How much bread do you have?" They responded, "Seven loaves and a few fish."
>
> He told the crowd to sit on the ground.
>
> He took the seven loaves of bread and the fish. After he gave thanks, he broke them into pieces and gave them to the disciples, and the disciples gave them to the crowds.

> Everyone ate until they were full. The disciples collected seven baskets full of leftovers.
>
> Four thousand men ate, plus women and children. After dismissing the crowds, Jesus got into the boat and came to the region of Magadan.

Ask:

- What speaks to you in this telling of the feeding of the four thousand? What questions do you have?
- Which story of using church resources in an innovative way spoke to you? Which did not resonate with you?
- What are some challenges that come with repurposing or letting go of traditional church buildings? What are some of the opportunities?
- How can we ensure that decisions about a faith community's buildings are guided by the Holy Spirit and aligned with our mission?
- How do your congregation's resources currently serve your community? How would you like to see them used?

Read this quote, followed by a time of silence:

"Generations do not cease to be born, and we are responsible to them because we are the only witnesses they have."[3]

Invite your group to look at the resources on your board then cup their hands and hold them out in front of them, imagining holding all those resources named at the beginning of your time together, as a leader prays:

"All that we have and all that we are is from you, O God. Make us stewards of your resources so that we may witness well to our neighbors and the next generations. In the name and courage of Jesus, we pray. Amen."

---

[3] James Baldwin, "Nothing Personal," in *The Price of the Ticket: Collected Nonfiction 1948–1985* (Boston: Beacon Press, 2021), 400.

Session 3: Blessing Our Neighbors, Growing Communities

(Chapters 5 and 6)

Welcome each person. Give thanks to God for the unique way each person loves God, their neighbor, and themselves. Ask each person to tell which story of holy disruption from these chapters inspired them most. Encourage them to truly retell the story in their own words.

Read the scripture passage Mark 12:28–34, taking turns reading a verse aloud at a time:

> One of the legal experts heard their dispute and saw how well Jesus answered them. He came over and asked him, "Which commandment is the most important of all?"
>
> Jesus replied, "The most important one is *Israel, listen! Our God is the one Lord, and you must love the Lord your God with all your heart, with all your being, with all your mind, and with all your strength.*
>
> The second is this, *You will love your neighbor as yourself.* No other commandment is greater than these."
>
> The legal expert said to him, "Well said, Teacher. You have truthfully said that God is one and there is no other besides him.
>
> And to love God with all of the heart, a full understanding, and all of one's strength, and to love one's neighbor as oneself is much more important than all kinds of entirely burned offerings and sacrifices."
>
> When Jesus saw that he had answered with wisdom, he said to him, "You aren't far from God's kingdom." After that, no one dared to ask him any more questions.

Ask:

- What are some tangible ways your faith community currently shows love to your neighbors? In what ways are you building communities of care? How could you imagine expanding that work in innovative ways?

- What seemingly impossible needs or challenges are your neighbors facing in your community?
- When, if ever, have you experienced help from a faith community when you needed it?
- What partnerships exist already for addressing the needs of neighbors in your community? What partnerships are lacking?
- If you could do anything to bless your neighbors or grow a community of compassion in your neighborhood, what would it be?

Read this quote, followed by a time of silence:

"The question which has to be put to every local congregation is this … whether its common life is recognizable as a foretaste of the blessing which God intends for the whole human family."[4]

Pray by imagining it is five years from now. Together, make up a story that your faith community might tell in the future about how you are transforming your neighborhood. What if your faith community is in the next book of stories about holy disruptors? Write down your story or record the telling of it on a cell phone. Add illustrations or anecdotes to really flesh it out.

Close by having a leader share this prayer:

"God who gave us our sacred story by moving into our neighborhoods in Jesus Christ, we ask that you make a story out of us that gives you glory and blesses our neighbors. Amen."

---

[4] Lesslie Newbigin, quoted in Chris Seay, "The Gospel, Church, and Culture According to Lesslie Newbigin," Ecclesia, November 3, 2019, https://ecclesiahouston.org/liturgy/2019/11/3/gospel-church-culture-newbigin.

Session 4: Dismantling Unjust Systems

(Chapter 7)

Gather some plants with roots you can see—ideally, one for each participant—and display them around you.

Open by asking participants to name issues in your local community that have been in the news recently, such as crime, illiteracy, or health issues. Ask: What are the roots of these problems? For example, if there are children in our community without enough healthy food to eat, what causes that? Allow for open discussion.

Read the scripture passage Luke 12:16–21, 31, taking turns reading each verse aloud:

> Then he told them a parable: "A certain rich man's land produced a bountiful crop.
>
> He said to himself, What will I do? I have no place to store my harvest!
>
> Then he thought, Here's what I'll do. I'll tear down my barns and build bigger ones. That's where I'll store all my grain and goods.
>
> I'll say to myself, You have stored up plenty of goods, enough for several years. Take it easy! Eat, drink, and enjoy yourself.
>
> But God said to him, 'Fool, tonight you will die. Now who will get the things you have prepared for yourself?'
>
> This is the way it will be for those who hoard things for themselves and aren't rich toward God."
>
> Instead, desire his kingdom and these things will be given to you as well.

Ask:

- What are some of the unjust systems the holy disruptors in this chapter are challenging?

- What does the parable of the farmer with an abundant harvest teach us about the use of our own resources within our current systems? Brainstorm together what the farmer might have done instead of hoard.
- What is one takeaway from these system-changing stories that you feel led to apply to your own life or to your community's efforts to promote the healing of the world?
- How do the examples of innovative ministries described in this book challenge our traditional notions of "church"?
- If God were to speak directly to my community, to me, commissioning us to work with God for the freedom and healing of a group of people oppressed by an unjust system, who would God be talking about in my community? In what ways does your congregation participate in current systems of the world, and in what ways do you offer an alternative to them?

Reflect by reading this quote, followed by silence:

"True compassion is more than flinging a coin to a beggar. It comes to see that an edifice which produces beggars needs restructuring."[5]

For prayer, ask your group to touch a root of a plant. Invite anyone who wishes to pray silently or aloud for the healing of the world at its roots. Then close by having a leader share this prayer:

"O God our Creator, Redeemer, and Sustainer, just because it is hard and overwhelming to change the world, don't let us give up on starting somewhere, loving someone, and doing something. Give us creativity and courage beyond what we think possible, all the way down to our roots. In the name of Jesus our Holy Disruptor we pray. Amen."

---

[5] Martin Luther King Jr., "Beyond Vietnam—A Time to Break Silence," sermon April 4, 1967, at Riverside Church, New York City.

Session 5: A Truly Hopeful Church

(Chapters 8 and 9)

Open by singing a favorite song or two from your faith community together. Then ask each person to share something they think is an essential part of being a church. Use your board to capture responses in sketches or words.

Read the scripture passage Acts 2:42–47, taking turns reading each verse aloud:

> The believers devoted themselves to the apostles' teaching, to the community, to their shared meals, and to their prayers.
>
> A sense of awe came over everyone. God performed many wonders and signs through the apostles.
>
> All the believers were united and shared everything.
>
> They would sell pieces of property and possessions and distribute the proceeds to everyone who needed them.
>
> Every day, they met together in the temple and ate in their homes. They shared food with gladness and simplicity.
>
> They praised God and demonstrated God's goodness to everyone. The Lord added daily to the community those who were being saved.

Ask:

- What, if anything, challenged you from these chapters?
- What are some key differences between focusing on institutional maintenance and focusing on embodying the message of Jesus?
- How does the relationship between your congregation and your denomination impact the decisions you make about the future of your institution?

- What is the difference between an "eschatology of destruction" and an "eschatology of hope"?
- What do you believe about where our world is headed and how God is at work in it?
- How does the story of St. Liborious Church and New Roots Urban Farm illustrate the idea of "hopeful disruption"?

Reflect by reading this section of a poem, followed by silence:

> This blessing
> will not fix you,
> will not mend you,
> will not give you
> false comfort;
> it will not talk to you
> about one door opening
> when another one closes.
>
> It will simply
> sit itself beside you
> among the shards
> and gently turn your face
> toward the direction
> from which the light
> will come,
> gathering itself
> about you
> as the world begins
> again.[6]

Ask participants to hold out their arms, as if they are holding a space for hope. Then pray together, saying the Lord's Prayer aloud in the way that is familiar to you.

---

[6] Jan Richardson, "Blessing When the World Is Ending," *The Painted Prayer Book*, July 18, 2016, https://paintedprayerbook.com/2016/07/18/blessing-when-the-world-is-ending/.Permission to reprint from Jan Richardson.

Session 6: Becoming Holy Disruptors

Open by sharing ideas of holy disruption opportunities that have come to you during this study. Encourage everyone to share something with the normal rules of brainstorming. No judgments, just creative juices flowing. Capture by recording, sketching out, or writing down this cacophony of creativity.

Read the scripture passage Ephesians 3:20–21 in unison:

> Glory to God, who is able to do far beyond all that we could ask or imagine by his power at work within us; glory to him in the church and in Christ Jesus for all generations, forever and always. Amen.

Ask:

- The parable of the sower is the story of generously planting seeds (resources) without knowing exactly what they will produce. What does this parable have to teach us, the Church?
- Which of the chapter's suggestions do you think is most helpful to your congregation? Which do you think may not apply to you? Which are you already doing?
- What does it mean to you to "trust in resurrection"? Tell stories of times when you experienced God bringing forth new life from death.
- How will you become a holy disruptor in the way of Jesus? How will your congregation?
- What are the specific, tangible steps we will take from here to keep walking in faith together?

Read this portion of a poem, followed by silence:

> Awaken your spirit to adventure;
> Hold nothing back, learn to find ease in risk;

Soon you will be home in a new rhythm,
For your soul senses the world that awaits you.[7]

Offer this prayer together, asking participants to raise their hands if they so wish when the prayer says "here I am":

"Grace-filled God, we want to tell a story that brings glory to you and hope to your people. Show us how to become holy disruptors as we trust anew in your resurrection power. We offer ourselves and our faith community to you. Here I am, send me *(pausing a moment for hands to be raised).* Make of us storytellers for your gospel, whatever it takes, we pray, in the name of Jesus. Amen."

---

[7] John O'Donohue, "For a New Beginning," in *To Bless the Space Between Us: A Book of Blessings* (United States: Doubleday, 2008), 14. Permission to reprint from Penguin Random House.

Acknowledgements

Thank you to the Invested Faith Fellows who allowed us to connect with them and capture a glimpse of their courageous stories. They are busy, gifted people who offered time and editing skills with generous spirits.

Thank you to Anita Flowers and her ministry of organization and connection, and especially for originally writing the stories of Invested Faith Fellows you can read at InvestedFaith.org.

Thank you to Brad Lyons at Chalice Press for trusting us with a resounding yes to publishing this book and to our editing team there.

Thank you to our invaluable readers along the way, Rev. Dr. Joe Weaks, Rev. Dr. Todd Adams, and the Rev. Drs. Victoria and Mark White, along with the insightful comments of our test groups, especially the First Presbyterian Book Group in Midland, Texas.

Thank you to our adult kids for their ideas and support and for whom we really, really hope the Church can evolve and keep thriving.

Especially, thank you to the congregations we serve, Community Church of Honolulu, Hawaii, and Connection Christian Church of Odessa, Texas, for being our encouragers always.

Appendix

About Invested Faith

Invested Faith is a legacy tool and a nonprofit fund created to allow churches, institutions, and individuals to reimagine the way faith communities can work to heal the world even after their institutional lives have reached their completion.

The contributed assets of these institutions and individuals are held in a growth fund and distributed in small, unrestricted grants to faith-rooted social entrepreneurs working to build businesses that become new models of faith community and justice-making across the country. We call these generous contributors "Invested Faith Partners."

Those investments begin generating immediate, practical returns because Invested Faith connects these funds to the work of social entrepreneurs who are building businesses working to dismantle unjust systems and heal communities.

These social innovators, called Invested Faith Fellows, receive a small, unrestricted grant from the Invested Faith Fund and can now, as of this writing, be found in twenty-two states and the District of Columbia working to address systems of injustice. The funding and support Invested Faith Fellows receive become integral to their success and thriving.

Invested Faith Fellows are world changers, and Invested Faith is the bridge that connects your gifts to their work.

The Invested Faith idea of small, unrestricted grants to faith-rooted social entrepreneurs is based on the teachings of Jesus, who kept inviting those around him to see the world with new eyes filled with possibility, to scatter seeds of goodness and justice with abandon, fueled by hope. Invested Faith has seen this model pay off over and over as we watch our Invested Faith Fellows thrive.

Some Invested Faith Partners are organizations reaching the end of their formal institutional lives. Thriving congregations also participate in the work of Invested Faith because they are excited about the mission and vision of Invested Faith and want to join efforts supporting this future-looking and faithful work across the country. Every contributor to the Invested Faith Fund is helping to build a vast network of innovative world-changers whose work will take what we invest now long into the future. Invested Faith is a new model for individuals and institutions to participate in justice-seeking work across the United States.

Invested Faith Thriving Church Partners are active and vital congregations participating in the work of Invested Faith because they are excited about the vision of Invested Faith and want to join efforts supporting future-looking and faithful work across the country. These gifts are grown and distributed as small, unrestricted grants to faith-rooted entrepreneurs dreaming up new models of community and justice-making across the country.

Thriving Churches contribute at all levels. With these gifts, churches and other faith institutions participate in the resurrection work God is doing in our world through their support of Invested Faith Fellows. Thriving Churches understand that their gifts have impact long beyond an initial investment.

Legacy Churches are congregations nearing the end of their life together. Often these churches face countless hurdles while grappling with the reality that their community will not continue on as it has been. At Invested Faith, we believe the work of healing the world continues, even as the institutions we've known and loved for so many years face the reality of ending a traditional institutional life. Through Invested Faith, the legacy of these communities lives on, honoring the past while seeding the future.

Individual contributors are often people who hold considerable wealth and understand that the religious institutions we have come to depend upon as social safety nets are serving us with less and less impact and effectiveness. These individuals know that holy disruptors working on the ground may now have some of the most critical impact at this moment in the life of our country.

Learn more and find ways you can support Invested Faith at www.investedfaith.org.